DALE EARNHARDT

The Intimidator

Dale Earnhardt: The Intimidator

Published by: Beckett Publications
15850 Dallas Parkway
Dallas, TX 75248

Printed in the United States of America

ISBN:1-887432-59-0

Cover photo by Tim Mantoani/Upper Deck

10 9 8 7 6 5 4 3 2 1

Corporate Sales and Information (972) 991-6657

By The Staff of Beckett Publications

Plus

GM
Parts
Goodwre
3
76
SIMPSON
plasti-kote
JE
Maxx
Rookie
of the
Year

NIGEL KINRADE

TABLE OF CONTENTS

Ralph
8
JR.
SPEED
Racing
KANNAPOLIS

COURTESY OF THE EARNHARDT FAMILY

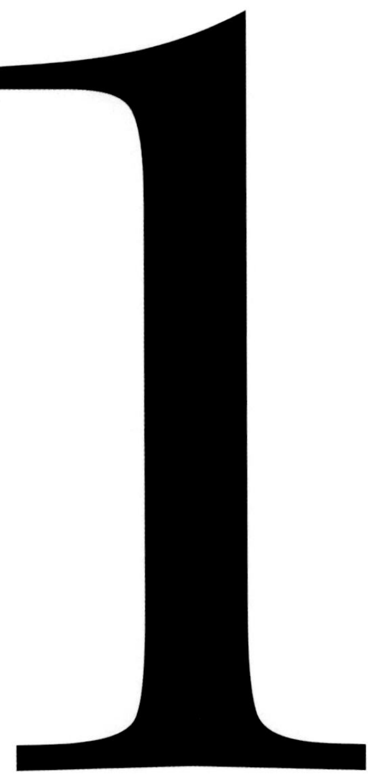

First Gear

Dale Earnhardt's earliest memories revolve around racing, and he grew up idolizing his father the stock car driver. No wonder all he ever wanted to do was race.

By Bruce Martin

Martha Earnhardt can't get over it. Sometimes, she'll be watching television, and there's Dale Earnhardt — her little boy — in a commercial. Or sometimes, she'll be shopping at the local grocery store in Kannapolis, N.C., and there's the face of her little boy on the side of a can of SunDrop or on the front of a box of cereal.

It seems that her son, Dale, is all grown up and one of the biggest things in NASCAR Winston Cup racing. In the process, he's become the source of a mother's abundant pride.

Martha and Ralph Earnhardt's first son in one of his first public appearances.

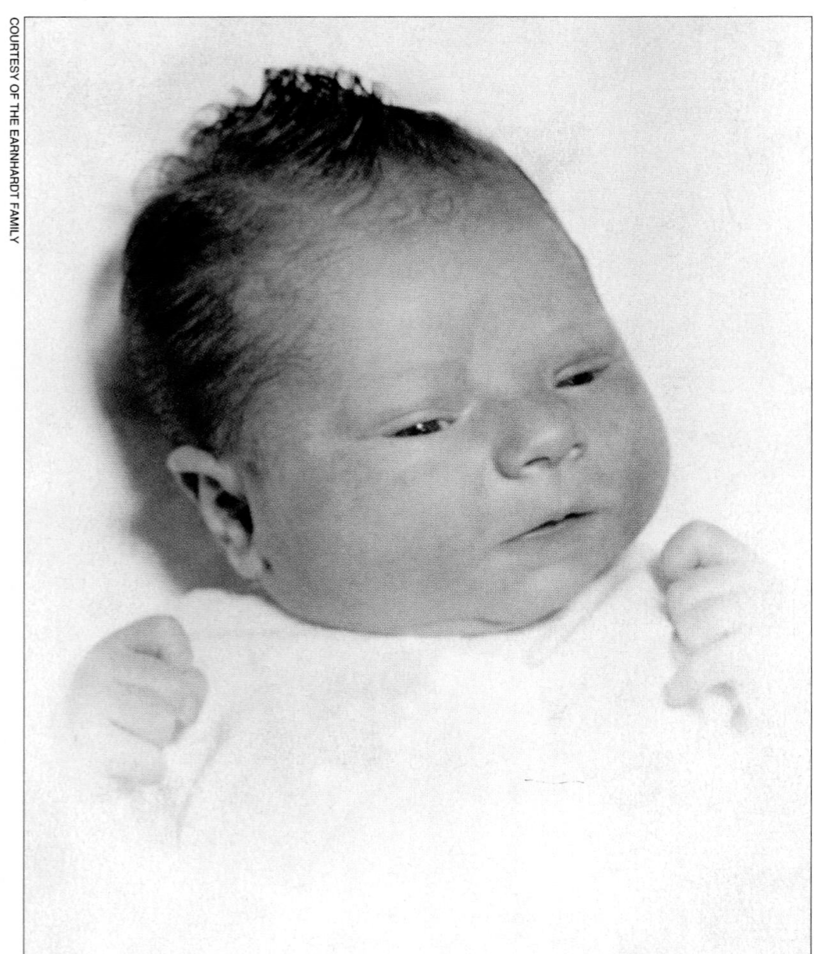
COURTESY OF THE EARNHARDT FAMILY

"It is really awesome for me sometimes when I look at the TV and there's my son in a commercial," Martha Earnhardt says. "Everywhere you look, there he is. I go into the grocery store, and there he is on a cereal box.

"It's hard to comprehend sometimes how far he really has come."

The eldest son of Martha and the late Ralph Earnhardt, young Dale was just like any other kid when he was growing up with his two sisters — Kathy and Kay — and two brothers — Danny and Randy — in Kannapolis, a textile mill community located 25 miles northeast of Charlotte.

"The kind of child Dale was with me, being my first son, I think his dad accused me of spoiling him a little bit," Martha admits.

As a boy Dale Earnhardt played baseball, football and basketball. But anything that involved cars really intrigued him. His father was a race driver, a legend in the NASCAR Late Model Sportsman Division (now known as the NASCAR Busch Grand National Series).

Young Dale idolized his father, and when he wasn't off doing kid things, he eagerly helped his dad in his race shop, located in the garage next to the house on Sedan Avenue in Kannapolis.

From the late 1950s through the mid-1970s, Dale enjoyed an easygoing lifestyle, and he relished it.

"When I didn't have to get up and go to school, I would hang around the neighborhood with the guys down at the creek or play in the woods," Dale says. "We would race bicycles and work on go-carts. I was always tearing something apart and trying to put it back together again. I was always tinkering.

The house where Dale and his four siblings were raised, at the corner of Coach and Sedan streets in Kannapolis, N.C.

CANDACE HYDE

CANDACE HYDE

Even Dale's most ardent fans would be hard-pressed to recognize the future Winston Cup champion at age 1.

"I played ball in the backyard and over across the road in the field. I didn't play Little League — I didn't have time for that. I went to the races on Saturday night and watched my Dad race.

"When I got big enough to help Dad," he adds, "I washed tools and washed race cars. This is when I was 7, 8 or 9 years old. I would pick up stuff for him, hold stuff or hand him stuff."

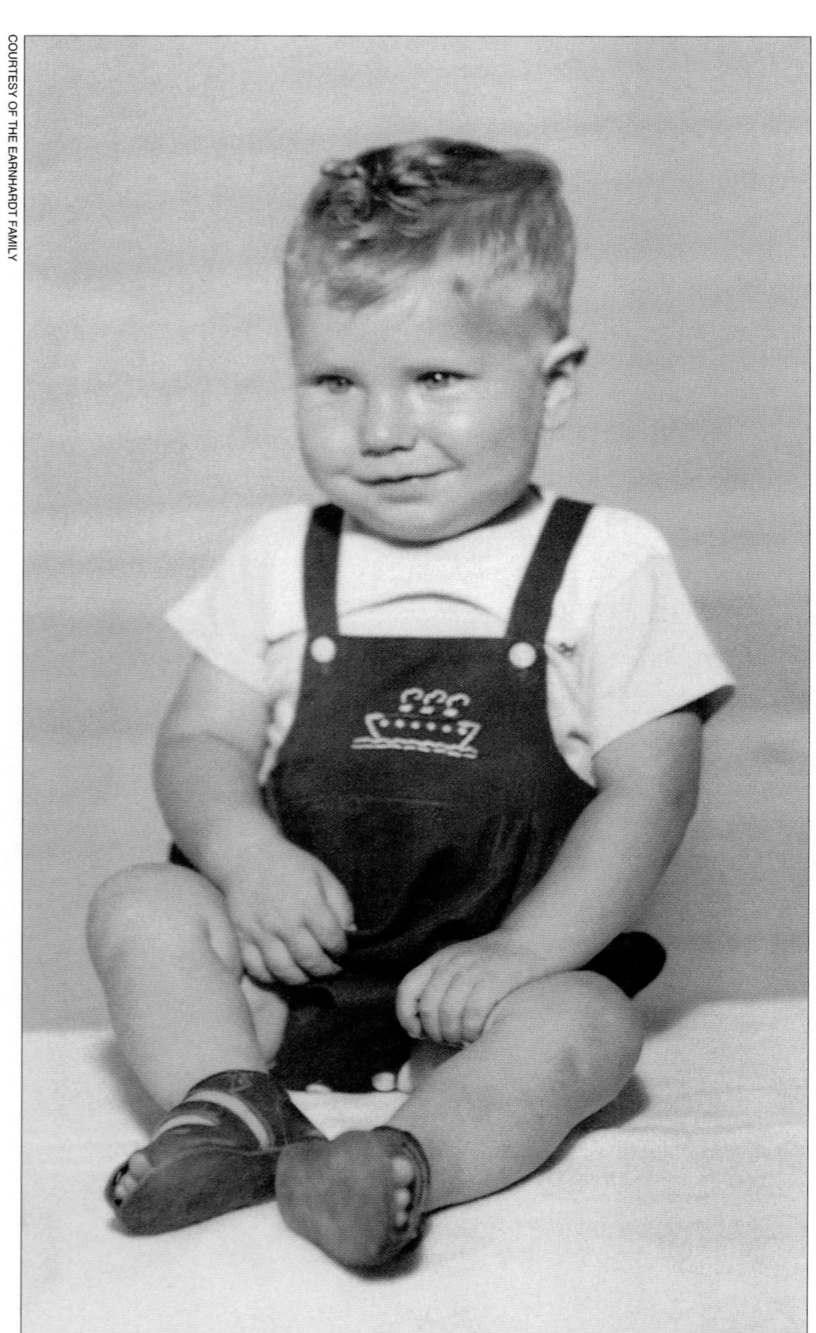

COURTESY OF THE EARNHARDT FAMILY

Dale Earnhardt's first recollections of watching his father race are among his earliest memories.

"I remember going to Hickory Speedway in Hickory, N.C., when I was just a little bitty kid," Earnhardt recalls. "I was 5 or 6 years old at the time. I remember going to Columbia Speedway [in South Carolina] when I was 10 or 12 years old and they wouldn't let me stay in the pits because they wouldn't let anybody under 16 in the pits back then. There was an old scorer's stand inside the fence inside the infield. I would sit on it and watch the race.

"When the officials would get busy with the heat races, I would slip back in the pits and get on Daddy's truck. Then, the officials would come by after every race and run me back out of the pits. That's when I would go to the truck down in the corners where Joe Whitlock and Jim Hunter [two Columbia sportswriters] and a lot of the old guys hung out and watched the race from back in them days. I would bum Pepsi-Colas off them.

"Mostly, they had beer, but I would dig around and get me a Pepsi. Then, I would bum a quarter off one of them and get me a hot dog."

Dale knew how to have fun at home in Kannapolis, too. One of his favorite activities was putting model race cars together, and he was an avid slot-car racer. He also enjoyed learning how to build transportation by himself — anything from bicycles to go-carts.

"I used to rummage around the rich neighborhood on one side of us," Earnhardt says, "and I would go scrounge wheels, frames, tires —

Although Dale's mother, Martha, doesn't like her son's image as an intimidating driver, the gaze of the man in black can indeed be an impressive one.

whatever I could scrounge and build me a neat bike. It would be a 24-inch frame with 20-inch tires on it, stuff like that."

The best thing about those homemade wheels was they provided him with something to race.

"We had a racetrack we raced bikes on," Earnhardt recalls. "Then, we got into go-carts. The rich kids down the street had three-speed English bikes then. They could beat you a little bit, but they couldn't beat you when you got to the corner because you would run over them and tear their wheels with the little, bitty tires on them.

Tires clearly weren't as important on Dale's earliest modes of transport as they are on his vehicles now.

COURTESY OF THE EARNHARDT FAMILY

"Daddy built us a go-cart out of tubing and car parts and whatever, and we raced that around the neighborhood. It was the neighborhood go-cart because when we got it out, everybody would be standing there wanting a turn. We had a big time on that thing."

JUST AS NOTHING SEEMS to faze Dale on the racetrack, little scared him as a youngster.

"I would ride a bike, climb a tree, whatever," Earnhardt says. "If somebody else tried it, you had to try it, too. We used to have a big tree on a huge bank that went out over the bottom and then over the creek. The creek had a little bit of running water in it. So we dammed the creek up so we could swing up there and dive into it. But nobody would do it to start with because they weren't sure the water was deep enough.

"I did it first," he recalls. "It was just barely deep enough. It took me a little bit to get up, so we built the dam higher the next time."

Dale at age 7.

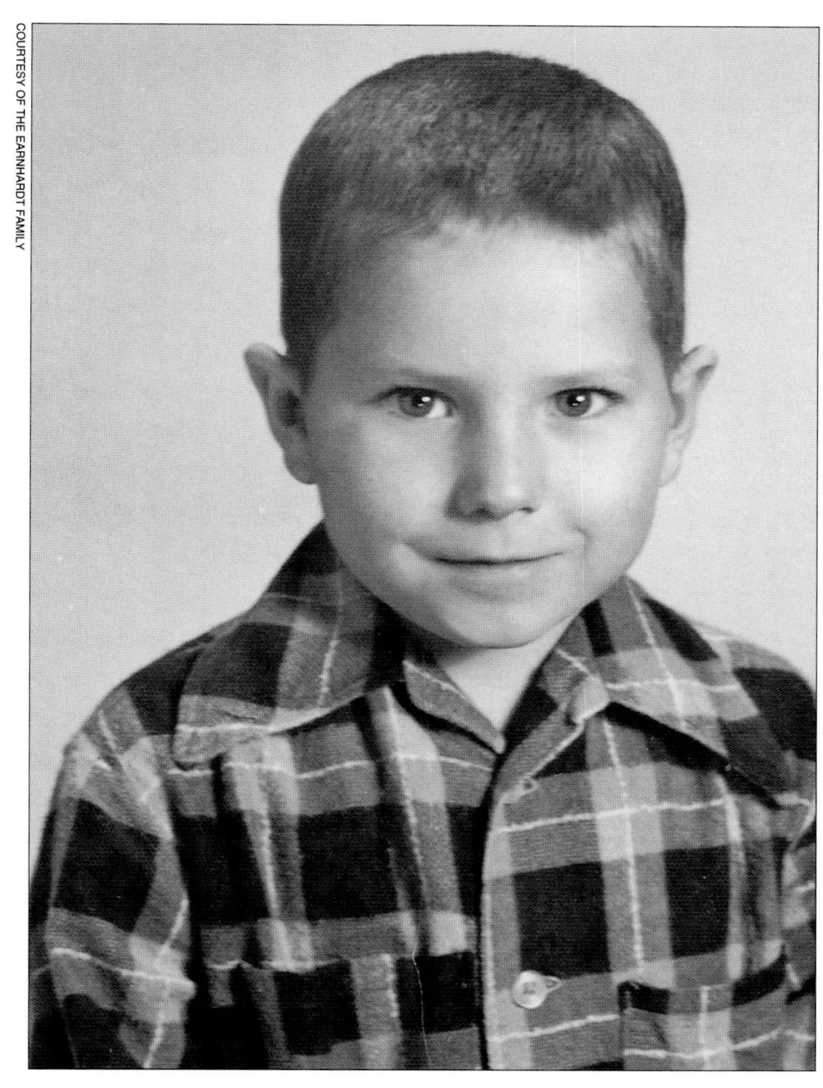
COURTESY OF THE EARNHARDT FAMILY

LEARNING HOW TO DRIVE came early for Earnhardt. He remembers driving tractors and trucks on his uncle's farm when he was 10 years old. Dale would drive the truck while his uncle and cousins would throw bails of hay onto it or put grain in a bin.

But for fun, Earnhardt would often skip playing ball to do what he loved best — racing.

"After supper, all the neighborhood kids would get together and you would time each other to see who could ride around the block fastest on a bicycle," Earnhardt says. "It was always competitive stuff like that. Or who could run the fastest, the farthest.

"We played ball, and we played football all the time around the neighborhood, but we were always racing something, too."

Although Martha says none of her children ever caused anyone much trouble, Dale did discover how to drive his older sisters crazy.

"He used to give his sisters a terrible time, especially their boyfriends," Martha admits. "Boys would come to the house to see the girls and Dale would aggravate them to death. They would try to catch him and they never could.

"He loves to aggravate anyway. His dad was a lot like that. Dale used to give his sisters a fit. Him and his brothers used to fight. You know how brothers are. They wouldn't fight, but wrestle and pick at each other. As long as you didn't pick on them.

"If you picked on them, he would fight you for them."

Loyalty always has been an important quality to Dale Earnhardt.

Dale's roughhousing never expanded beyond the Earnhardt house, though. "I never had any trouble with him getting into fights or anything like that at school," Martha says. "He wasn't a bad kid at all. He was a good kid. All of my kids were good. I'm proud of them all."

That's why, even today, Martha Earnhardt takes exception to Dale's image as an intimidating race driver — the man in black.

As a young boy in Kannapolis, Dale enjoyed the company of his brothers and sisters, neighborhood kids and the family dog.

COURTESY OF THE EARNHARDT FAMILY

"I think they have carried that too far," Martha says of Dale's image. "It makes me mad sometimes the way they portray him. It hurts me as a parent. I don't care how old your child gets, he is still your child. Any time anybody says anything bad about him or derogatory about him, it hurts me.

"I've tried to make myself get used to it, but it is still hard to do."

While Dale always enjoyed a close relationship with his mother, to this day he proudly states that his father had the biggest influence in his life.

"My dad is why I'm here," Earnhardt says. "My dad was the focus of my life. I didn't like school. I wanted to be

home working on Dad's race car. I wanted to be home working on cleaning up the shop. I would just as soon be washing wrenches. I followed him around and did everything he did."

By watching his father race, young Dale learned a lot of lessons he would apply once he began his own racing career.

Dale loved tagging along when his father (car No. 8) raced at local tracks such as Concord Speedway, as is evident from the pride on his face while posing with one of his father's trophies.

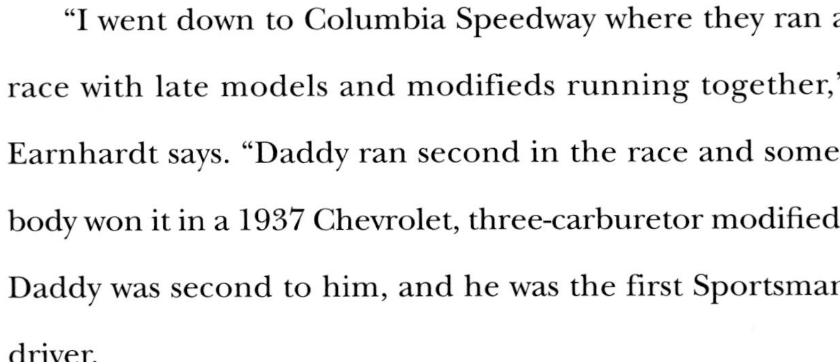

"I went down to Columbia Speedway where they ran a race with late models and modifieds running together," Earnhardt says. "Daddy ran second in the race and somebody won it in a 1937 Chevrolet, three-carburetor modified. Daddy was second to him, and he was the first Sportsman driver.

COURTESY OF THE EARNHARDT FAMILY

COURTESY OF THE EARNHARDT FAMILY

"I was so impressed with him running second, I walked up to the cars on the racetrack, where victory lane was. I would always check the air pressures on Daddy's tires after the race. I would feel the hubs and stuff, and he was never hard on the brakes. That's why the hubs were cool.

"I walked up to Gerald Moss' car and the left front was a funny color. I stuck my fingers to that thing. I reckon he had used a lot of brakes on the modified to get it stopped.

"I was smarter than that already, but I burnt my hand all to heck. I was 12, and I burnt my hand on that thing. I thought, 'Boy, if he was hard on brakes, I would hate to work on his car,' because I knew how much service we did on Daddy's car.

"I remember asking Daddy on the way home, why the brakes were so hot on [Moss'] car. He said it was left-foot braking. I started to learn about brakes and driving with and without the brakes, so when I started racing, I already knew all that kind of stuff about using brakes.

"I never used much brakes, but that is learning the hard way — hands-on type of things."

YOUNG DALE ALWAYS STRIVED to make his parents proud, but there's one thing he did in life that made them angry. To this day, he recalls it was one of the dumbest things he ever did.

Dale quit school. It made his father so angry, he wouldn't speak to his son for weeks.

"I wasn't happy at all," Martha says. "We begged and pleaded and tried to cajole him into going back to school. We offered to buy him a car. We tried to bribe him in any way we knew to go to school.

"He would go to school — he was not a bad student. He didn't cause any problems in school. He just didn't learn a lot because he wasn't paying atten-

While waiting for his racing career to take hold, Dale worked at Punch's Wheel Alignment. The owner told Dale he'd go broke.

CANDACE HYDE

tion. He would be thinking about cars and stuff like that."

Despite the fact he now admits making a mistake in quitting school, he showed he had learned the value of responsibility when he went to work at Boulevard Sunoco on Highway 29 in Kannapolis when he was 16.

"The guy who ran it and who I worked for, he worked a lot of hours and I worked a lot of hours," Earnhardt recalls. "He got killed in a car wreck. After he got killed, I ran the station for about a month-and-a-half, two months by myself more or less. I had afternoon help pumping gas, but I ran the station as far as opening it and running it and money in and out every day. I was 17 when that happened.

"One week, I worked 70 hours. It was the longest week I pulled in that entire time. It was something else." In the process, he earned back the respect from his father that he had lost by quitting school.

"You had to earn responsibility and respect from him," Earnhardt says. "Daddy was an independent person. He was a hands-on type laborer. He worked for everything he got, and it didn't come easy. I didn't get an allowance when I was growing up. When I needed money, I got it [myself].

"I reckon we were average, working-class people, but I never knew money was an issue. I always thought we had plenty."

Dale has come to appreciate the lessons he learned from his father, because Ralph Earnhardt no longer is here to give his eldest son advice.

One day in 1973, Dale walked into the race shop to

find his father slumped over the car. Ralph Earnhardt had died of a heart attack at age 44.

Dale used to race in the streets of Kannapolis when he was growing up. Now, one of those streets is named after him.

"I was so mad at him for leaving this world, I didn't get over it for a year," Earnhardt admits. "I'm still not over it. There isn't a day that goes by that I don't think of my father."

Martha Earnhardt believes Dale took his father's death probably harder than anyone else in the family.

CANDACE HYDE

"I think mainly he regretted not taking his dad's advice about a lot of things and not going to school and finishing," Martha says. "He realized, after his dad was gone, how much his dad tried to teach him and he didn't really pay enough attention.

"You know how young people are — sometimes they think they know more than you do. All young people are like that. [Dale] wasn't the only one — all of my children were.

"[Ralph's death] hurt all of my children, and they still miss their dad even though it has been so many years since he died. I guess with Dale being into racing and wanting to race, he really missed him worse because he knew that when Ralph died, it took a lot of the knowledge of racing away from him because he wasn't there to give him advice and to help him through what he wanted to do."

With his father gone, Dale knew he would have to summon an inner strength to carry on in his absence. With a racing career on the horizon, Dale went to work at Punch's Wheel Alignment in nearby Concord, N.C.

"Dale was pretty straightforward," recalls Punch's son, Punchy Whitaker. "He was pretty knowledgeable on cars. He was no-nonsense and got the job done.

"He was just like one of the guys. He had a good head on his shoulders. He was always real witty and cutting up and stuff.

"But all Dale talked about was wanting to go into racing. My father told Dale at the time he went racing that he was going to go broke.

"I think he missed that call."

A framed check signed by Dale Earnhardt is on display in Punchy's office. "It was a payroll check for $205 for two weeks, and that was after taxes," Punchy says. "But that was in 1974. Things were different then."

That amount pales in comparison to the millions Earnhardt now earns both on and off the racetrack.

But despite the luxuries that come with the money and the adulation, Dale Earnhardt longs for those simpler days of his childhood in Kannapolis.

"Dale told me one day, 'Mom, I wish I didn't have to do anything but get in that race car and drive it, "Martha says. "I told him, 'Son, you shouldn't have been so good at it, you wouldn't have had to worry about it.'

"He just wants to drive a race car. That is all he wanted to do in his life — drive a race car."

Bruce Martin is the national auto racing writer for United Press International and a neighbor of Dale Earnhardt in Mooresville, N.C.

DAYTONA RACING ARCHIVES

Driven to Succeed

Dale received his formal education on the back-road tracks of the Carolinas as he single-mindedly pursued his passion for racing

By Benny Phillips

DAYTONA RACING ARCHIVES

After the war, at the height of its virility, when its jaw was clean and its stomach flat, the state of North Carolina could hardly wander past a mirror without stopping to admire itself.

The boys were home from foreign soils, and textile and furniture factories were running two, sometimes three, shifts. There wasn't even a rumor that cigarettes might cause cancer, so agriculture boomed, and tobacco became the No. 1 cash crop.

The image the state saw of itself was good, even progressive.

Every town had minor league baseball, and fans — still reluctant to spend meager wages on out-of-state travel — packed the stands and foul lines for home games.

A few sports entrepreneurs, such as they were, analyzed the turnout at baseball games. Sufficiently insightful to recognize a new generation's love for the automobile (and its horsepower), these men, many of them swashbucklers of the highest order,

His father Ralph, who often had broken bones to show for his efforts, was Dale's role model as a parent and a race car driver.

envisioned another form of competition that might attract paying customers. So in short order, farm machinery began turning corn, cotton and tobacco fields into small dirt bullrings called racetracks. Sawmills hummed to produce enough rough boards for the grandstands, fences, ticket booths and concession stands.

Racetracks popped up like drive-in theaters, and soon there was one of each within easy driving distance of any town. Like drive-in theaters, though, most of the racetracks eventually folded. The reasons were numerous, but the word "lack" was used in every explanation — lack of organization, lack of insurance, lack of publicity, lack of drivers, lack of money.

Anyway, Bill France Sr.'s NASCAR, then only in its infancy, would eventually resolve most problems for track survivors. But meanwhile, the small outlaw tracks spawned many of today's top names in Winston Cup racing: Petty, Wood, Johnson, Jarrett,

DAYTONA RACING ARCHIVES

Dale picked up much of his mechanical knowledge from dad Ralph (right), who often worked on cars with friends Cotton Owens (left) and David Pearson.

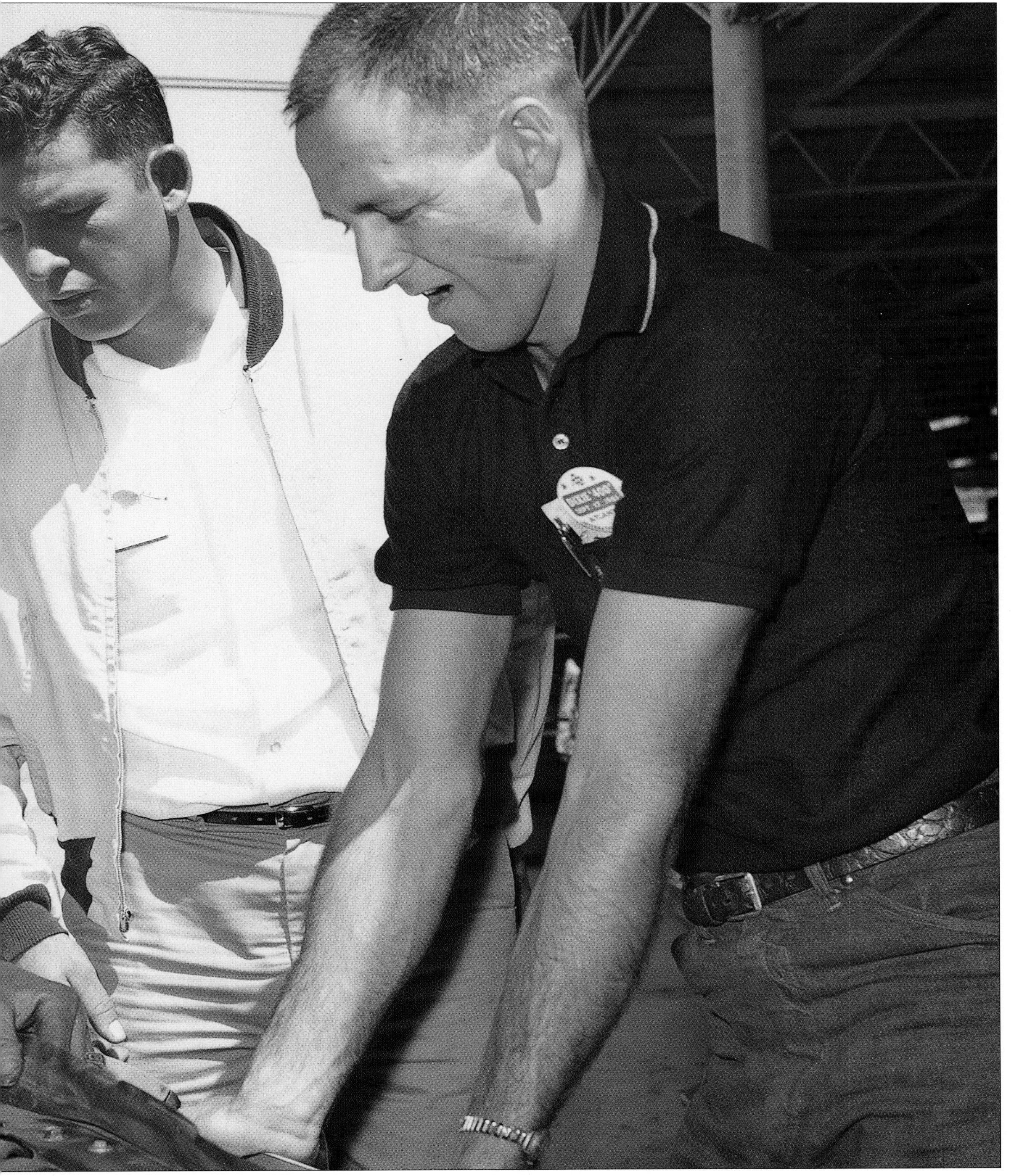

Allison and — yes — the ever-intimidating Earnhardt.

Ralph, national Sportsman champ in 1956, earned the respect of his peers for his determination and intensity.

"When Ralph started racing," begins Martha Earnhardt, "our oldest daughter was 5 months old. I had most of my kids pretty quickly, and she was 14 months when our next daughter came along.

DATONA RACING ARCHIVES

"We had a little Ford coupe and the seats folded down. We put a bassinet behind the seat with one daughter in it, and I held the other one in my arms.

"After Dale came along," she continues, "we had to slow down. We didn't have room in the car for another baby."

That is how Martha Earnhardt, Dale's mother, remembers the early days when her husband, Ralph, raced in those years following the war.

Ralph and Martha raised two daughters and three sons on what racing produced in the way of income. They did it from a small car shop (by today's standards) in the textile town of Kannapolis, 20 miles outside of Charlotte.

Ralph Earnhardt won the national late model Sportsman championship in 1956, beating Ned Jarrett by 570 points. He raced anywhere somebody waved a green flag, and won several track championships. But perhaps more importantly, the man who died of a heart attack at age 44 in 1973 left a legacy of being among the toughest to wear a racing helmet.

"If there's ever been a chip off the old block, it's Dale Earnhardt," Jarrett claims. "Ralph Earnhardt was the most intense, hard-driven man I have ever known."

Dale Earnhardt, born April 29, 1951, had just turned 22 when his father died. He did not understand his father's death, nor did he accept it for a long time. Even after joining the Winston Cup circuit full-time in 1979, Dale talked often and proudly about his father. Mostly he told racing stories, but sometimes Dale talked about hunting and doing other things with the man he loved so dearly.

"After he passed away, I went quail hunting but once the next year," he said in '79. "And the day I went, everywhere I looked, he was there — the dogs, the guns, the old memories of us hunting together.

"It was the same way in the shop. I'd go there to work on my race car. I'd need a wrench or a certain part or I'd catch myself turning and sometimes almost asking him how to do something.

Dale first became acquainted with Daytona when he raced Sportsman cars there in the mid-'70s.

DATONA RACING ARCHIVES

"And sometimes I'm sure his spirit rides with me in my race car, as sure of it as anything in the world."

Dale's hero remains Ralph Earnhardt, as it has been from the beginning.

"I would wash and clean up his race car before I left for school," Dale recalls. "It would be late when he'd get home, and he wouldn't be up yet. I'd have things ready for him at the shop when he got up."

Dale, who began racing late model, six-cylinder stock cars at age 15, finished the eighth grade and started the ninth, but quit school at age 16 to devote himself to the life he loved.

During the time Dale was running the six-cylinder cars on dirt tracks, he occasionally enjoyed the privilege of racing against his father. The father and son drove against each other just a couple of times, but Dale particularly remembers an encounter one night at Metrolina Speedway near Charlotte.

The late model Sportsman field, the division Ralph Earnhardt raced in, did not have enough cars for the feature event. Track officials determined that in order to have enough cars for the feature event, the top five finishers from the lesser, six-cylinder division main event would start at the rear of the field in the late model Sportsman feature. Dale, his mind set on earning a spot in the field against his father, won the six-cylinder race, so he was among those who started in the rear of the field in the late model Sportsman main event. Having worked his way to fourth, Dale looked in his mirror and saw Ralph Earnhardt, the race leader, coming up to lap him.

He pulled over to let his father pass, but Ralph pulled right in on his rear bumper. In fact, he began bumping Dale every now and then. Dale picked up the pace and when he approached the third-place car, Ralph pushed him right on by and into third place. Then Ralph passed Dale and drove away to victory with the Earnhardts finishing first and third.

"There was a big stink after the race," Dale recalls. "The driver we passed claimed the Earnhardts ganged up on him."

Dale continued to pick up Sportsman and Winston Cup rides through 1978. The next year, he joined Terry Labonte (center) and Joe Millikan (right) in the rookie class of 1979.

Before he started racing on his own, Dale would go with his father to the small tracks of the Carolinas. "I remember one night in Columbia, S.C., Dad was racing Dink Widenhouse for first or second," Dale remembers. "They got together, and Dad went over the bank in Turn 1. There were billboards down there, and you could hear the engine still running and every now and then see one of the billboards shake. Dad came back up the bank and onto the track in Turn 2 and lost just two positions."

CHOBAT RACING IMAGES

CHOBAT RACING IMAGES

After his father's death, Dale drifted about from track to track, pulling his own rig, working on his own race car, a loner so to speak. He kept the race shop open and worked on his race cars there. He crossed the

A
B
16
Winston
Cup
Official
GM
Goodwrench
Service
MONTE CARLO
3
UNOCAL
GOODYEAR
76
COMP
SIMPSON
plasti-kote
SPRAY PAINT

peaks and valleys of his career during these years, sometimes borrowing money at the bank on Friday afternoon, knowing he didn't have enough to cover the loan, but knowing he had to do well enough racing on Friday and Saturday nights to deposit what he owed on the loan early Monday morning before the note came due.

DAYTONA RACING ARCHIVES

"My daddy would never have approved of me borrowing money to race," Dale says. "He didn't do business that way and would have fussed at me."

Dale's career on asphalt began in 1974 in a 5-year-old Sportsman car he'd bought from Harry Gant. He achieved some success against Sportsman veterans such as Tommy Houston (the uncle of his future wife, Teresa) on smaller tracks. Later that year, he entered the 300-mile Sportsman race at nearby Charlotte Motor Speedway, his first competition at a high-banked track. He finished 13th.

The following May, Earnhardt entered his first Winston Cup race, the 1975 World 600 at Charlotte. In an Ed Negre-owned Dodge, Earnhardt started 33rd and finished 22nd, one position ahead of Richard Childress.

Through 1976 and 1977, Dale continued Sportsman racing while begging occasional Winston Cup rides. Struggling and in debt, Earnhardt in 1978 took a wrecked Chevrolet rebuilt by Rod Osterlund's crew to Charlotte in October and finished second in a Sportsman race.

Cale Yarborough (center) and Lee Petty (right), who ran son Richard's team, were among Dale's earliest NASCAR rivals.

Earnhardt then ran the Dixie 500 in Atlanta for Osterlund and finished fourth. The plan was for him to drive a second car for Osterlund in 1979, but after Dale drove for Osterlund in the Winston Cup season-ender at Ontario, he was asked to drive the full Winston Cup schedule in 1979.

DALE NEVER WON TRACK championships like a lot of drivers because he kept moving. Sometimes, it turned out best that way.

One night he might race at Columbia, Greenville or Myrtle Beach and the next night at Concord, Hickory or wherever he felt good about going. Some places he wasn't welcomed back, but he took things in stride, the good with the bad. He grew up understanding that racing wasn't for the meek.

For example, on one particular warm, summer evening during his late model Sportsman career, he drove slowly through the shadows of Caraway Mountain, towing his race car to Caraway Speedway near Asheboro, N.C. Caraway was Sam Ard's home turf. Nobody much beat Ard at this half-mile track unless Ard had mechanical failure. He drove for the family who owned the track, and all three rings of the circus featured Ard.

Earnhardt raced at Caraway only occasionally. On this night, he was the tall stranger who rode into town with a big iron on his hip, there to do business.

They didn't make conversation before the race. Earnhardt looked Ard over from a distance. He knew the situation. Ard stared at Earnhardt occasionally. He didn't seem too concerned. The previous week Harry Gant had come to Caraway and left with a second-place finish, and the week before that, Jimmy Hensley drove down from Virginia and finished second. Sam Ard was a good race driver, especially on his home track, and the occasional hot dogs who came to Caraway seldom ran in front of him. He didn't figure this Earnhardt kid from Kannapolis would be any tougher than the rest, although he did remember Ralph Earnhardt and how hard he used to drive.

The mechanical know-how passed from Ralph to Dale Earnhardt has helped the Intimidator keep track of things at each and every pit stop.

CITGO
UNOCAL
Goodwrench Service
MONTE CARLO
SIMPSON
3

Ard started from the pole in the feature, and soon Earnhardt trailed by only a car length. As the race progressed, Ard maintained the lead as Earnhardt tried to pass time and again, inside and outside.

On the last lap. Earnhardt tapped Ard gently in Turn 1 and tried to go inside. Ard kept his mount under control and maintained the lead until he reached Turn 3. It was there that Earnhardt ducked to the inside and plowed his way by, using his car like a bulldozer pushing aside snow on some northern freeway. Ard spun into the outside wall, and Earnhardt took the checkered flag. Ard's disciples booed Earnhardt profusely.

Earnhardt and Ard pulled into the pits at about the same time. Each got out and the two stood toe-to-toe shouting obscenities at each other. But never a lick passed, nor did one put a hand on the other. The dispute never seemed to faze Earnhardt. He obviously never took into consideration that he was outnumbered probably a thousand to one. If he did hear his heart beating in his throat, he concealed his feelings well. He gave the appearance of someone willing to take on all comers, if necessary. Whatever the cost of the ticket to victory lane, he was willing to pay it.

Earnhardt encountered problems at various tracks and with different drivers, but survived as he knew he would. His father gave no quarter on the racetrack and taught his son to do likewise.

"Daddy told me when I caught somebody, I shouldn't stay behind them more than two laps. Daddy's theory was that if you can run down and catch another driver, you can pass him — somehow."

Dale accelerated his professional development by racing as often as possible on the Busch circuit.

These days, Earnhardt races only Winston Cup and IROC (International Race of Champions) cars. He quit the Busch Grand National division following the 1994 season to concentrate on winning a record eighth

BUSCH
Dale Earnhardt
union
CHAMPION
NASCAR
Winston Cup
DAYTONA INTERNATIONAL SPEEDWAY
WINNER
BUSCH CLASH OF '80

Winston Cup championship.

The Busch circuit had been good for Earnhardt. When NASCAR decided to overhaul its late model Sportsman division and rename it Busch Grand National in 1982, Earnhardt won the first event, the Sportsman 300 at Daytona, a preliminary to the Daytona 500, the major event that had eluded him until his victory in 1998.

Ultimately, he won seven Busch races at Daytona, including the last five Goody's 500 races in which he participated. In capturing the 1986 race, Dale honored the memory of his late father by driving car No. 8 — the car number Ralph Earnhardt rode to a national Sportsman championship in 1956 — into victory lane.

From 1982 through 1994, Dale ran 136 Grand National events. He won 21 races and seven poles. He posted 17 of his 21 victories on superspeedways, and he ranks fifth all-time in victories in this division. Jack Ingram heads this list with 31 victories, followed by Tommy Houston with 24 wins, and Ard and Tommy Ellis with 22 each.

Incidentally, Earnhardt's winnings in the Grand National division

SCOTT CUNNINGHAM

In honor of his father, Dale drove a No. 8 car to victory when he won his second Grand National race at Daytona in 1986.

amounted to more than $900,000. Needless to say, by the time Dale left the Busch circuit, he no longer had to worry about making a beeline to the bank on Monday mornings to pay off his debts.

Benny Phillips is a sportswriter for the *High Point* (N.C.) *Enterprise*.

Goodwrench
1994
Winston Cup Champions
Winston Cup Series
NASCAR
Simpson
Goodwrench

1994

CHOBAT RACING IMAGES

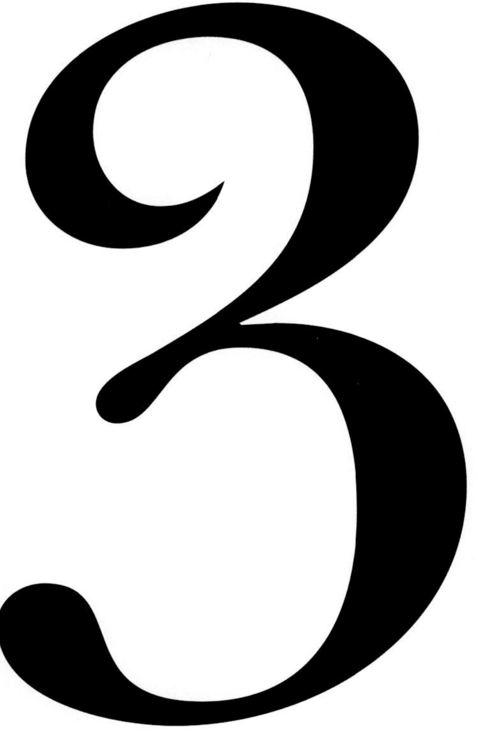

No Holding Back

Undeterred by changes in ownership or the ruffled fenders of his peers, Dale chased success with relentless determination and ultimately became the dominant force in Winston Cup racing

By Bob Zeller

When he looks back at his first race in the NASCAR Winston Cup series, which occurred more than 20 years ago, Dale Earnhardt sees a raw, rough kid who had no business doing what he was doing — yet was utterly driven to do it anyway.

He remembers with awe and fascination how he somehow qualified for the World 600 at Charlotte Motor Speedway in 1975. He was 24 years old, and he'd run on a big speedway only once before. His first race in the big leagues would be NASCAR's longest, toughest event.

"I was probably the most confused and excited person in the country that day," Earnhardt recalls. "I had never run anything over 200 laps on a racetrack, and here I was going to run 600 miles [400 laps] at Charlotte."

CHOBAT RACING IMAGES

As a Winston Cup rookie in 1979, Dale benefited from the experience of veteran crew chief Jake Elder.

CHOBAT RACING IMAGES

Richard Petty won that day. Dale finished 45 laps down, in 22nd place. No doubt there are no other 22nd-place finishes in Earnhardt's career he is so proud of.

Twenty-two years, seven championships and nearly 600 races later, Dale is considered one of the finest drivers in the Winston Cup series. But his first race at Charlotte proves that even the best have to start somewhere south of the victory lane.

"I worked hard driving Ed Negre's car that day," Earnhardt recalls. "It was a 1974 Dodge. The car weighed about 4,000 pounds, no power steering. It was really a bear to wrestle around the racetrack. One of my last pit stops was for water.

"I was burned out. But I made it all the way. And it was a pretty exciting day for me," he adds. "I didn't realize at the time what my part in racing was or where I was going. I just wanted to race."

Dale's first trip to victory lane — the 1979 Southeastern 500 at Bristol.

DOZIER MOBLEY

The most vivid memory Earnhardt owns from that race is of Petty, who finally broke his 15-year 600 jinx that day.

"I'm wrestling that car and no one is in sight," Earnhardt remembers. "I go into Turn 1 and no one is in sight. I go through Turn 2 and no one is in sight. I'm going down the backstretch and I can't be a car length off the wall and all of a sudden, Richard Petty passes me on the outside. I don't know how he got through there. There wasn't that much room, and he about threw me off the racetrack."

The Atlanta 500 marked the first of Dale's five victories in 1980, the year of his first Winston Cup title.

CHOBAT RACING IMAGES

An even lesser-known fact about Earnhardt's first race is that when the race finally ended, another driver was on the same lap as Earnhardt, also 45 laps down. Finishing 23rd, one spot behind the newcomer, was longtime journeyman driver Richard Childress, who later would create the team that provided the home for Earnhardt's greatest successes.

From that inauspicious start, Dale Earnhardt embarked on a long, difficult road to success in the Winston Cup series. His life in racing actually got much tougher before it got easier.

In 1976, Earnhardt found two rides in the series. One was in the World 600, where his engine failed, and the other was in the Dixie 500 held in November at Atlanta. There, driving Johnny Ray's Chevrolet, Earnhardt experienced a frightening accident in which the Chevy flipped end over end after slamming head-on into the spinning wreckage of Dick Brooks' car. Earnhardt luckily suffered no serious injuries.

CHOBAT RACING IMAGES

At Charlotte Dale posted his first hometown victory. He finished the 1980 season under Wrangler sponsorship.

Earnhardt scrounged only one ride in 1977. His race in the fall event at Charlotte ended after 25 laps when his rear-end gear failed.

By 1978, Earnhardt was heavily in debt from his short track pursuits. But he was forging friendships with Winston Cup people and looking for breaks. He got one that May, inheriting a ride in the World 600 in Will Cronkrite's car when scheduled driver Willy T. Ribbs failed to show for two practice sessions. Earnhardt finished the race 17th — with relief from Harry Gant.

He ran at Daytona in July for Cronkrite and finished

CHOBAT RACING IMAGES

seventh, then finished 12th at Talladega and 16th in the Southern 500.

His exploits piqued the interest of California businessman and car owner Rod Osterlund, who offered Earnhardt a ride in the Dixie 500 at Atlanta in November. Earnhardt qualified 10th, just behind regular Osterlund driver Dave Marcis. In the race he finished fourth, again just behind Marcis. It was an impressive debut.

By finishing fifth at Riverside, the unlikely pair of Dale and 20-year-old crew chief Doug Richert (left), captured the 1980 points title.

AP / WIDE WORLD PHOTOS

"I'd sure like to keep this ride," Earnhardt said after the race. "I think in time I could win with this car."

In December, when Osterlund offered him a full-time ride for 1979, Dale finally captured the break he'd been looking for. And he was determined to reward Osterlund for his gamble.

EARNHARDT WASTED LITTLE TIME establishing himself as one of the rising talents in stock car racing. He led 10 laps in the 1979 Daytona 500 — his first laps led in a Winston Cup race — and finished eighth. In March, veteran crew chief Jake Elder, especially effective with young drivers, joined the Osterlund team. Things were coming together.

At North Wilkesboro, Earnhardt led again — late in the race — before finishing fourth. And at Bristol, on April Fool's Day in 1979, Earnhardt won his first race. It was just his 16th start.

That day, he started ninth and grabbed the lead for the first time on lap 139. He led laps 255 through 388 and then passed Darrell Waltrip with 25 laps to go. He won by 3 seconds.

"I'll probably believe it in the morning," Earnhardt said in victory lane. "This win was in the big leagues. It was against top-caliber drivers. It wasn't some dirt track back home."

Dale's joyride careened off course when car owner Rod Osterlund (bottom, left) abruptly sold his team in 1981.

CHOBAT RACING IMAGES

And then he backed up his victory with a string of consistent finishes — the same formula that ultimately led to so many of his Winston Cup championships.

In May, he placed fourth at Nashville, fifth at Dover and third in the 600 at Charlotte, where he and Richard Petty swapped second place three times in the last lap. He ran sixth at Michigan, third at Daytona in the 400 and third in the return visit to Nashville.

Earnhardt and crew chief Kirk Shelmerdine were a good fit, but Dale and car owner J.D. Stacy weren't — their union lasted four races. Dale finished the 1981 season driving for Richard Childress, a recent competitor (Childress in white car).

On July 30, he was leading at Pocono when a tire blew and he pancaked the wall with the driver's side of his Chevy. Earnhardt broke his collarbone and suffered a concussion and numerous cuts and bruises. Most troubling to him, though, was the fact that his injuries could cost him his ride.

David Pearson took over for four races and won the fourth one — the Southern 500 — in dramatic fashion. The next weekend, Dale was back behind the wheel, winning the pole in Richmond. He finished fourth, with relief from Lennie Pond, and declared afterward, "I'm glad this ride is mine again."

He wrapped up the 1979 Rookie of the Year title with several more strong

CHOBAT RACING IMAGES

CHOBAT RACING IMAGES

CHOBAT RACING IMAGES

finishes, including a second place at Atlanta, where Neil Bonnett passed him with four laps to go. It was his first run at the Winston Cup championship. He had finished seventh, again just ahead of Richard Childress.

Dale's two years with Bud Moore and Ford unfortunately produced too few victories and too many DNFs.

JUST FOUR DAYS INTO the 1980 season, Earnhardt signed a five-year contract to drive for Osterlund. Here was the security he'd been looking for. Osterlund was a man he could trust, and a man who trusted Dale. The personal bond, which now seems so important to Earnhardt's success, had been established.

CHOBAT RACING IMAGES

Earnhardt ultimately won five times in 1980. And even though Elder left after the World 600 in May and was replaced by 20-year-old Doug Richert, the transition was all but obscured by the results.

He won the Busch Clash, and started the season with four straight top-five finishes. Dale already led the points race when he copped his second career victory at Atlanta in March. The points lead was his for good.

"This I could get used to," he said in victory lane at Atlanta. "This beats the heck out of any other feeling I've had recently."

He won the next race, too, successfully defending his title at Bristol. In July, he captured a win at Nashville. And in the stretch run, he won at Martinsville and at Charlotte, giving him five victories that year.

At Atlanta in November, which was the penultimate race in 1980, Earnhardt staged a side-by-side duel with race leader Cale Yarborough in the final laps, even though Earnhardt was a lap down. Yarborough, who was chasing Dale in the title race, was furious.

This wasn't the first time Earnhardt would be accused of rough driving, nor would it be the last. But it was one of the first prominent incidents, and while it turned many fans against him, it attracted just as many new ones.

In the season's final race at Ontario, Calif., Earnhardt finished fifth, winning his first title by 19 points over Yarborough despite a dangerously bungled pit stop late in the race. The race ended with Earnhardt circling the track with just two lug nuts on his right rear tire. Still, he managed to hang on to fifth.

Soon after winning his first championship, Earnhardt began paying some of the dues he'd skipped during his meteoric rise to stardom in NASCAR racing.

Dale didn't win a race in 1981. Of greater significance, Osterlund sold the team in midseason — to Earnhardt's shock — to eccentric coal baron J.D. Stacy. From the start, Stacy didn't sit right with Earnhardt. So Dale left Stacy after four races and joined forces with Childress, who quit driving to field a car for Earnhardt.

They enjoyed moderate success — a couple of fourth-place finishes — but Childress knew he did not yet have the capability to field championship-

Reunited in 1984, the team of Earnhardt, Shelmerdine and Childress won for the first time at Talladega in July.

DAYTONA RACING ARCHIVES

FIRST UNION
FIRST 400
1995 WINNER
NORTH WILKESBORO SPEEDWAY
North Carolina U.S.A.
QUICKLUBE plus
NASCAR Winston Cup Champion
RCR
SIMPSON RACE PRODUCTS
GM
dwrench
ice
goodwrench service

caliber cars for a championship-winning driver. He urged Earnhardt to join veteran Ford car owner Bud Moore for the 1982 season.

Earnhardt won at Darlington in April, but he failed to finish a staggering 18 races. In 1983, Earnhardt won twice, including his first victory at Talladega, and finished eighth in points. But he still recorded 13 DNFs.

Earnhardt got along with Moore, but Dale said he never managed to build a comfortable relationship with Ford. In 1984, he rejoined Childress. He won two races that year and finished fourth for the title. A team was beginning to gel.

In 1985, Earnhardt won four times, but finished eighth in points. In 1986, it all came together, although sometimes with a crash. His second title also brought bitter accusations of rough driving. A new and sometimes controversial era in Earnhardt's career had arrived.

SCOTT CUNNINGHAM

Well before his run to the 1986 title, Earnhardt often endured criticisms of rough driving. But the incidents took on a new tenor in 1986. Most of the races were now televised live, and NASCAR racing was really beginning to take off. By then, Earnhardt stood as one of the top stars. Everything he did on the track was magnified larger than life for millions of TV viewers.

At Richmond, in just the second race of the year, Earnhardt was involved in one of the most controversial incidents of his career. With three laps to go, Darrell Waltrip passed Earnhardt coming off the second turn. Going into the third turn, Earnhardt stuck the nose of his car where there was no hole and clipped Waltrip's right rear quarter panel. The ensuing crash snared all the drivers on the lead lap except Kyle Petty, who won the race.

Earnhardt was fined $5,000 and placed on a year's probation. The probation

During the mid-'80s Dale became notorious for his aggressive driving style, the consequences of which periodically were evident on his car.

later was dropped and the fine was reduced to $3,000. Earnhardt pleaded that he'd made a mistake, but that he did not intentionally wreck Waltrip.

Powered by four victories, as the stretch run began in 1986 Dale held a solid 141-point lead over Waltrip. Once again, as in 1980, he withstood the championship pressure in stride, winning at Charlotte and clinching his second title with a victory at Atlanta. He beat Waltrip by 288 points.

The following campaign was Earnhardt's finest year, but it was his most

AP / WIDE WORLD

tumultuous as well. If he wasn't driving past his competitors, he was driving through them. He won 11 times, but he made many enemies en route to victory lane. In the long run, the notoriety enhanced his reputation as a renegade, one of the most popular attributes for a stock car racing star, and heightened his marketability.

Earnhardt won at Rockingham and again at Richmond, but there he spun Harry Gant out of the lead. "He ran all over me," Gant said at the time. "He's done that before, though. It's not really a surprise."

Earnhardt swept the spring short track swing, winning four in a row to put an early stranglehold on the title.

In May came his controversial victory in The Winston, one of the roughest races in recent NASCAR history. As the final segment started, Earnhardt tapped Geoff Bodine and sent him spinning out of the lead. Dale and Bill Elliott then slugged it out.

Despite his hard driving reputation, Dale has had few serious wrecks. He walked away from this one at Pocono in 1982.

AP / WIDE WORLD

Earnhardt, Childress and their wives celebrated their first Winston Cup championship together in 1986.

With seven laps to go, Elliott nudged Earnhardt and forced him through the grass in the tri-oval. But Earnhardt held his lead and went on to win. Afterward, both Elliott and Bodine were so mad at Dale, they rammed his car (on pit row).

But Earnhardt had won the race. In a fight with cars at 170 mph, he proved

DOZIER MOBLEY

he was the toughest driver on the track that day.

The seventh of his 11 victories in 1987 came at Michigan in June. Victory No. 8 was at Pocono in July, where he nudged Alan Kulwicki out of the groove, and out of the lead, on the last lap.

And then Earnhardt claimed three more in a row — Bristol, Darlington and Richmond — by which time he'd built a staggering 608-point lead over Bill Elliott. Dale eventually won by 489 points. He failed to finish just two races that year and posted 21 top-five finishes in 29 races.

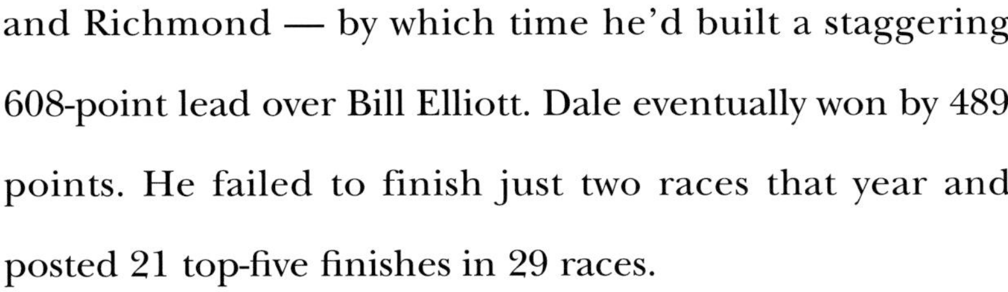

In 1988 and again in 1989, Earnhardt ran in the title hunt, finishing third in 1988, behind Bill Elliott and Rusty Wallace, and second behind Wallace in 1989.

As the final decade of the 20th century started, Earnhardt was poised to dominate his sport like no other driver before him.

The titles fell like dominoes in the 1990s. Childress, so well-versed in the ways of racing, had assembled a skilled, satisfied, motivated team. And behind the wheel sat a driver who had developed into the finest racer ever.

The rough driving, for the most part, was behind him. Between 1990 and 1994, just Terry Labonte and Bill Elliott were involved in fewer yellow flag incidents than Earnhardt.

The formula for winning titles became classic — a quick start (despite Earnhardt's well-chronicled failure to win the Daytona 500 until 1998), a steady flow of mostly top-five finishes, a few poles, a few victories and a determined run down the stretch to the championship.

Winston Cup titles in 1987, 1990 and 1991 established Dale and the RCR team as NASCAR's dominant team force.

In 1990, Earnhardt whipped Mark Martin. In 1991, he vanquished Ricky Rudd.

In 1992 came the inevitable slump. He won only one race and finished 12th in points. Longtime crew chief Kirk Shelmerdine, who had guided Earnhardt to four titles, suffered burnout and left. From Harry Gant's team came crafty veteran Andy Petree to replace Shelmerdine, and the Earnhardt-Childress juggernaut regained its momentum.

CHOBAT RACING IMAGES

NIGEL KINRADE

In 1993, Earnhardt beat Rusty Wallace for the title, pounding him into submission with seven top-five finishes in the final 10 races. Dale entered the finale at Atlanta with a 126-point lead and wrapped up his sixth championship with a 10th-place finish. Among Dale's six victories that season were triumphs at Darlington, Charlotte, Daytona and Talladega.

And in 1994, after Ernie Irvan was injured at Michigan in August, Earnhardt lost his stiffest competition. At the time of Irvan's season-ending crash, he trailed Earnhardt by 27 points. Dale clinched his record-tying seventh title with a victory at Rockingham on Oct. 23, his fourth of the campaign. He eventually won the championship by 444 points over Mark Martin, the largest differential since Dale's 489-point margin over Bill Elliott in 1987.

A week after clinching, Earnhardt reflected on his remarkable team and his enviable record.

1990
Champion
GoodWrench Racing
Winston
GOODYEAR
RCR
Dale Earnhardt
Goodwrench
SIMPSON
76
AC
GM Parts
Winston Cup Series
NASCAR
1990
WINSTON CUP CHAMPION
DALE EARNHARDT

"Everybody on our team is important, but I'm going to tell you, the important man on that team is Richard Childress," Earnhardt said. "His preparation, his building and learning of the team, his placing people in certain positions, has made the team what it is. Richard Childress and I see things on the same wavelength."

In 1995, Earnhardt made a valiant bid for his record-breaking eighth championship. He held the points lead as late as mid-June, then fell behind Sterling Marlin and later Jeff Gordon before dropping as low as fourth overall. Even with victories at Indianapolis and Martinsville in the second half of the season, the best he could manage was a second-place finish behind Gordon.

With championships in 1993 and 1994, Dale finally caught up to Richard Petty's record of seven Winston Cup titles.

NIGEL KINRADE

NIGEL KINRADE

MINOLTA
SONY
U.S. NAVY 575-0606
U.S. ARMED FORCES
NO TURNS
AS YOU CAN GET
CLEAR FIRE LANE FOR EMERGENCY VEHICLES
TIMES SQUARE
CLEANER BRIGHTER SAFER
NASCAR RACE CAR
NASCAR Winston Cup
UNOCAL 76
BUSCH Pole Award
True Value HARD CHARGER
Gillette
Goody's HEADACHE POWDERS
CHAMPION
Holley CARBS
Western Auto
STP
Prestone
Gatorade THIRST QUENCHER
1

In '96, Earnhardt appeared to be on his way to an unprecendented eighth Winston Cup championship before a violent accident in the DieHard 500 at Talladega in his 18th race of the season that left him with a broken collarbone and sternum. Although he didn't miss much time behind the wheel, Dale never regained his early season form, which included wins in two of the first four races and nine other top-five finishes.

The next season, Earnhardt got off to a slow start, then suffered a bizarre turn of events at the Mountain Dew Southern 500 when his car twice nicked the wall on the first lap. Unable to complete a single lap, Dale was taken to the hospital and eventually determined to have had a migraine-like episode in which a blood vessel feeding the base of the brain went into spasm.

Earnhardt later said he remembered nothing, not even starting the race. For

He didn't win a record eighth Cup title in 1995, but in August Earnhardt did capture the second annual Brickyard 400 at the Indianapolis Motor Speedway.

BRIAN SPURLOCK

the first time since 1981, Dale didn't win a race, and he finished fifth in the Winston Cup standings, his lowest finish since 1992. The idea of a "disappointing" fifth-place finish in itself speaks volumes about The Intimidator's career, and the '97 season was virtually forgotten when Earnhardt won the most dramatic race of his career, the 1998 Daytona 500, marking his first win ever in NASCAR's version of the Super Bowl.

Looking back on what he's accomplished since joining the Winston Cup circuit full-time in 1979, "it's a pretty impressive record," he candidly conceded back in 1992. "Richard and I talked about it quite a bit. What's impressive to me in winning races and championships is the time we've done it in. I've raced in Winston Cup full time for 14 [you can now make that 19] seasons, and I've won seven championships. I can't imagine that.

"I'm amazed we've done what we've done. I'm not bragging or anything. I've just pretty much impressed myself."

Not to mention the wide world of Winston Cup racing.

Bob Zeller covers the NASCAR Winston Cup series for Landmark Newspapers: the *Norfolk Virginian-Pilot*, the *Roanoke* (Va.) *Times and World-News* and the *News and Record* in Greensboro, N.C.

UNOCAL
76
NASCAR
Simpson
RCR

CHOBAT RACING IMAGES

4

Partners for Life

Dale Earnhardt has forged a number of key relationships in his life and racing career, but none have been as important or fulfilling as the union he enjoys with his wife, Teresa

By Ben Blake

Dale Earnhardt Inc.

The man's name alone connotes success to millions of NASCAR fans and admirers of his many Winston Cup victories and seven series championships. The "Inc." reinforces the image — the same effect as if the capitalist icon were referred to as John D. "The Intimidator" Rockefeller Jr.

Dale and Teresa have traveled a long road together, from his earliest days in victory lane . . .

Dale Earnhardt Inc. is the primary company that manages Dale's wide-

DAYTONA RACING ARCHIVES

spread business interests. This mini-empire comprises Earnhardt's Busch and SuperTruck teams, his souvenir and appearance trade, a Chevrolet dealership in Newton, N.C., a poultry farm, cattle raising, rental and investment properties, an air-travel service — even a yacht charter business in Florida.

This side of Earnhardt embodies the fulfilled dreams of people like him: a small-town kid with little formal education who ventured into the world and succeeded on a grand scale. He's made considerable money in racing, and through shrewd use of it, he's built a conglomerate of close to 150 employees, which generates (estimates say) up to $40 million a year.

There's an old Southern saying: "I'd rather be lucky than good." Earnhardt has been both, the "good" abetted greatly by his good fortune. Dale has been most fortunate in his associations with good people.

Richard Childress, Earnhardt's car owner since 1984, indisputably is a winner. Earnhardt's crew chiefs have been Hall of Famer Kirk Shelmerdine, the talented Andy Petree and the well-respected Larry McReynolds. Dale's been surrounded by a Who's Who of mechanical talent — Will Lind, David Smith, Chocolate Myers, Danny Lawrence, Lou LaRosa, Ed Lanier, Bobby Hutchens.

. . . to a position in the sport where his place is unmistakably secure.

NIGEL KINRADE

But who is the one person most responsible for Dale's success?

"Teresa," Earnhardt responds, without blinking.

Teresa, of course, is Teresa Houston Earnhardt, his wife since 1982. The niece of veteran Grand National racer Tommy Houston, Teresa is a slight, pretty, soft-spoken woman with dark hair and big, dark eyes. Moreover, she's a sensible, get-to-the-point person who helped rough, young Dale Earnhardt evolve into Dale Earnhardt Inc.

DON HUNTER

Earnhardt always manages to find time for his family, but even away from the track, he occasionally has to tend to official business.

Teresa and Dale became acquainted at North Carolina racetracks around 1977, two years before he graduated from Sportsman racing to the elite Winston Cup circuit. After winning Rookie of the Year honors in 1979, Dale shot to the top of his profession in 1980, when he won his first NASCAR championship with car owner Rod Osterlund.

Osterlund and Earnhardt had what was said to be a five-year contract. But the mercurial Osterlund suddenly sold the team to J.D. Stacy midway through the 1981 season, leaving Earnhardt's future in jeopardy. That's when Dale learned to rely on Teresa's quiet good sense.

"When I first started, agreements and things like that weren't that important to me," he says. "Teresa and I sort of learned the hard way. The first time I got upset with things was when Osterlund sold the team and I had to go and get my business back from him. He'd handled all my affairs and sort of paid me an allowance. My personal things were all set up through him."

Earnhardt cited several lawyers and accountants who helped him through this difficult period, but "as far as making decisions, what team to be associated with or what associations with what sponsor, that was all done between Teresa and I, maybe with a little advice from close friends.

"She's just always had good sense," he continues. "She was very smart in school. And she'd been involved in businesses, so we more or less did it all for all these years. Teresa and I have been the ones that yea, nay and approve all this stuff."

Throughout the years, Teresa also has supervised and modified hundreds of agreements involving Dale and the likes of sponsors, trading card companies and souvenir sellers.

"Those are things you have to figure out over a period of time," she says.

When Dale feels like taking it a little bit slower than 150 mph, he steps behind the wheel of a different kind of vehicle.

DON HUNTER

"He and I knew what he was looking for, such as what kind of terms, and I would write those down and make up new contract clauses.

"I think sometimes going through a legal agreement can be confusing because of the wording," she adds. "Sometimes the parties involved try to use that to their benefit to try to confuse you. You could just let it go, and it could mean any number of things, depending on how you interpret it.

CHOBAT RACING IMAGES

Dale last shaved his mustache in 1983, for a Wrangler ad. His fans are more accustomed to seeing him pictured as he is on the opposite page.

"So we try to clarify them, take out the lawyer language and put in normal everyday words. Just simplify things, really."

EARNHARDT, THE NOTED TOUGH guy, visibly softens when he expresses his admiration for his wife.

"What appealed to me about Teresa, other than she's a good-looking lady, is, from Day One, I don't care if I was working on the car late at night, or racing and driving it home in the middle of the night — she was right there.

"Sometimes I'd work so late at the shop, I'd be too tired to drive, and she'd drive me home. We'd stop somewhere and get something to eat, or she'd fix us something.

"She'd go to school the next day, then work at her job. If I was still working on the car, she'd drive up from Charlotte to Kannapolis and help me on the car or drive me home."

Theirs largely was an unconventional lifestyle, but it was the only way for Dale to gain a toe-hold on the racing career he wanted so badly.

"I'd race at Metrolina Saturday night, then come back over to the apartment

Gatorade
GM
oodwrench
MOM 'N' POP'S
Snap-on.
CITY
YEAR
76
NASCAR
Winston Cup
Champion
RCR
rvice
Serv

and clean up. Then we'd put the Sportsman car on the trailer — it'd be 11 or 12 at night," he remembers.

Now the president of Dale Earnhardt Inc., Don Hawk (walking with Dale) manages Dale's myriad business interests, which range from his Chevrolet dealership in Concord, N.C., . . .

"We'd get in that truck — a one-ton, straight-drive truck — and she'd drive, pulling a race car. We'd drive out Sugar Creek Road, all the way out to [Highway] 74, down to Myrtle Beach. My brother lived down there at the time. I'd climb up in the sleeper and go to sleep.

"In the morning, Randy'd bring us out something to eat. We had it made. We'd hang out at the beach in the morning, go shopping, see the sights, come back at 2 or 3 o'clock, take the truck and go out and race at Myrtle Beach Speedway that night. Then we'd come back and spend the night with Randy, then go out and mess around on the beach on Sunday.

CHOBAT RACING IMAGES

"We didn't have a dime in our pockets, and we were just tickled to damn death."

Teresa clearly didn't marry her man for his bank account.

"We didn't have a lot of money between us," Dale says. "We got up one morning, and I knew we didn't have much groceries. She said, 'You want me to fix you something to eat before you go to work?' I said, 'We ain't got much, do we?' She said, 'I'll find something.'

SCOTT CUNNINGHAM

"She fixed me fried tomatoes, fresh tomatoes out of the garden and toast. And we didn't have nothing to drink but Lambrusco wine — for breakfast — and off to work we went."

Teresa's self-reliance is another quality that attracted Dale to her.

"She's always been that way," he says, then relates a story to illustrate his point. "She once busted a radiator hose coming home from work at River Hills Country Club just across the line from Charlotte in South Carolina. She had a Ford Pinto wagon she was driving.

"She pulls into a service station, steam coming up, and the hot light comes on. The guy comes out, raises the hood and says, 'You've got a split radiator hose. I'll run down to the parts store and get one.'

"She said, 'No, let it cool off a little.' She cracked the radiator cap, put some water in it, then got her gray tape out. She wrapped that sucker up, filled the radiator back up with water, left the pressure cap loose — she's smart enough to do that — shut the hood, and drove it back to the house.

. . . to souvenir sales that are the envy not only of NASCAR rivals, but all but a handful of professional athletes worldwide.

GEORGE TIEDEMANN / SPORTS ILLUSTRATED

WESTERN STEER
Snap-on
Goodwrench
SIMPSON
MOM'n'POP'S
RACING
TOOLS

"We're eating supper, getting ready to go to Concord Speedway, and she says, 'By the way, can you put a radiator hose on my car?' [Fixing the hose] was not a big deal to her. She didn't grab the phone and cry. She just patched her up and came on home.

"She's always been that kind of person," he says. "She'll work at a contract the same way — look through it and see where it takes us down the road."

In the 1990, Dale and Teresa have taken increasing control of Earnhardt assets and trademarks. They acquired Sports Image Inc., a Concord, N.C., company that had handled the licensing of Earnhardt merchandise.

Also, the Earnhardts hired Don Hawk, a whirling dervish of merchandising. Hawk, as slick and competent as they come, has progressed quickly from manager to vice president to president of Dale Earnhardt Inc. The addition of

Like their father, Dale's grown children from previous marriages — (from left to right) Kerry, Kelley and Dale Jr. — have found the lure of the track irresistible. Dale and Teresa's 9-year-old daughter, Taylor Nicole, is no stranger to the winner's circle, either.

CHOBAT RACING IMAGES

Hawk has kicked the Earnhardts' business machine into high gear.

"Dale and Teresa are very private people," Hawk relates. "In my interview process with them, I had to fly with them to a couple of races. I traveled with them to Pocono, and we interviewed for a whole weekend.

"We also went to Talladega — Dale won that race — and on the airplane coming back home, we finished everything up. They're really uniquely confidential people."

Away from the track, Dale finds relaxation pursuing deer from a hunting blind in the woods . . .

CHOBAT RACING IMAGES

The Earnhardts and Hawk constitute a powerful business triumvirate. In some ways, Hawk has assumed much of the contract drudgery that Dale and Teresa had to wade through previously.

"Teresa and I do 99.9 percent of their contracts," Hawk says. "There are very few we don't take and reword or redo. I bring it up to a stage where Dale and Teresa can sign it. Teresa may change one or two things, Dale may change one or two things, but normally when I get it to 'em it's about ready to go."

Dale Earnhardt Inc., meanwhile, has competent people in charge of each of its subsidiaries — the car dealership, the poultry farm, the racing teams. These managers don't need much supervision, Hawk says.

"If I wanted to, I could pick up the phone and call any of the places and say, 'What about this, what about that?' " Hawk says. "I don't because Dale Earnhardt surrounds himself with good people. He's got managers in each of those places doing their job well."

. . . or working with Teresa on their chicken farm in Mooresville, N.C.

SCOTT CUNNINGHAM

The difficulties women with children face in two-income society affects Teresa directly, but she doesn't make a big deal out of these issues. Like everything else, she takes them in stride.

"I tell [Dale] every day I'm as busy as he is," Teresa says, laughing. "But that's one good thing; at least being involved in it, as busy as I am, I can go along and make my own schedule."

Dale and Teresa have a daughter, 9-year-old Taylor Nicole. Dale also has three grown children by previous marriages — daughter, Kelle King, and sons, Kerry and Ralph Dale Jr. All three now have racing careers of their own — part of DEI's group of interests.

In the motor coach the Earnhardts use on the road, Taylor is ever-present, which is how Dale and Teresa like it.

"Even as busy as we are, we're together," Teresa says. "You always can take a minute or so to get a hug or whatever, listen to what [Taylor's] got to say or talk to each other.

"As long as you're happy, that's what's important anyway."

Teresa says she doesn't get nervous about her husband's risky occupation.

"I can't remember when I haven't been to a race he was in. It just makes me more comfortable when I'm there," she says.

"I don't get nervous really. I just get excited. I get anxious before the start. That's one thing that's gotten easier — the waiting before the race, all the time you have to kill. I used to get real anxious. Now, I just kill time. I bring a lot of things to keep me busy, too."

Dale and Teresa have come a long way from fried garden tomatoes to Dale Earnhardt Inc. It's been a lot of work, and success has come at a price.

"I don't know how we handle it," Dale says. "I can't keep up with my stuff — paperwork and mail. My autograph fan mail, I don't know if I ever catch up.

"I'm buried. I don't know how other athletes feel. It's their business how they treat the fans. I might be late getting something back to the race fans, but if it comes back to them, if my name's on it, I signed it — not a secretary, not another person. I signed it."

Teresa says the couple's friends are "people who understand we never get to see them, maybe just twice a year or three times a year."

PPG
NASCAR Winston Cup
QUICK LUBE
GOODYEAR
NASCAR Winston Cup Champion
RCR
76
AC
GM
Goodwrench Service
Winston

"We never took a vacation for like seven years because we were so busy traveling and so busy at home," Teresa said several years back. "It'll be interesting to see in five years what's going on. Maybe I'll be retired by then."

She says she wouldn't miss her present hectic life. These days, the couple enjoys getting away on their Hatteras yacht, putting in at remote Caribbean

MICHAEL C. HEBERT / SPURLOCK PHOTOGRAPHY

islands where Dale Earnhardt is just another guy on the beach.

"Dale's a good business partner, he really is," Teresa says. "But it's not anything either one of us really enjoys. It's the necessity, and it's hard to make time for that when you travel so much and you're not ever in the office.

"And when you're home, you have to take care of small, everyday things like laundry and meals, the things you've got to do just to live. You don't have time to do things that really need to be done, like contracts and approvals for pictures or whatever.

"You have to be a workaholic. I've always been the kind that wanted to get out of doing the work — now here I've been drawn into such a busy lifestyle that I have no time to do anything. So when we get away, I'm real good at just putting it totally out of my mind and just relaxing."

In his professional life, Dale has benefited greatly from another strong relationship. He and car owner Richard Childress won six NASCAR championships in 11 years. The number of championships they won relative to their time together is unmatched in NASCAR history.

The great marvel of the Earnhardt-Childress connection has been their sustained high level of performance.

Earnhardt turned 47 in April 1998, and Childress is 52. The two men have made millions of dollars in racing, and their interests and plans are following separate trails. Although their relationship has changed throughout the years, Dale and Childress share a deep-rooted kinship.

"Sometimes it's too close," Earnhardt says. "It's scary.

Dale's most enduring and successful professional relationship has been that with car owner Richard Childress, with whom he's shared six of his seven Winston Cup titles.

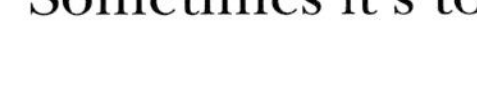

"It's hard to be close and friends with someone you're in business with, because people get upset about things sometimes. But I think that's what's helped Richard and I, because we are friends. We'll listen and hear each other out. We don't get mad and blow up and him go one way and I go another and sulk about it for a month, then, at the first little thing, blow up again.

"If something's bothering Richard or something's bothering me, we'll set each other down and talk about it. That's the best way. Sometimes you don't want to do it, sometimes you want to put it off, sort of ignore it for a while. But you can't do that."

CHOBAT RACING IMAGES

The friendship and the business relationship endured through the summer of 1995 as Earnhardt and Childress negotiated a contract extension. Their former arrangement carried them through 1996. The extension runs through 1999, likely the end of Earnhardt's driving career.

Childress admits it's harder these days to maintain the kind of relationship he and Earnhardt have enjoyed since 1984.

"We have a good relationship," he says. "We don't have any major problems.

"The difference is the sport itself. The amount of time we have to spend together now is a lot less than in '85 or '86. We used to talk and hunt and fish. Now he's gone this way, and I've gone this way.

"We've been able to separate the business side from the personal side. Today, there's just so much more of the business side than personal side because neither one of us

Andy Petree (right) had been part of Childress Racing's last two titles. But when Petree moved back to Robert Pressley's team, Earnhardt hooked up with respected crew chief Larry McReynolds for the 1997 season.

has the time we used to have."

Some have hinted that Earnhardt's overwhelming business interests have detracted from his attention to racing and to the Childress team. Earnhardt denies that, noting he gave up driving his Busch Grand National car (which he owns) in part to give more time to the Childress group.

"People talk about focus, and Childress and I sit down and talk about focus a lot," Earnhardt says. "The No. 1 thing that's important to me is how that No. 3 car runs. If I don't feel like I'm giving it the focus, I'll tell Richard that, or I'll change things to where it doesn't take away from that.

"The people who are close to me and know me can see that and understand

SCOTT CUNNINGHAM

that. The people sort of on the outside, team members, people involved with Richard, some of them question that sometimes.

"They'll have to come to terms with that. All I can do is drive the car like I'm doing. Results tell the tale."

As big as Earnhardt gets, he hasn't yet outgrown his britches. He still has great respect for his car owner, and he understands now the alchemy between himself, Childress and the team transcends what any one man can do.

"He took and built this team," Earnhardt says plainly. "You were talking about where I'd be, where he'd be. It's sort of like country singers Brooks and Dunn.

"They were both singers, both flogging it in the nightclubs trying to make it, and neither one was going anywhere. And they both interviewed with this same guy, different clients, and this guy put 'em together.

"He introduced them, and they got going and boom, they were a hit. Apart, they weren't nothing — I mean, not nothing, but they hadn't made it.

"It's the same scenario with Richard and I. I had been a champion, but I was more or less wandering out there.

Richard Petty once was Dale Earnhardt's idol. Petty always will be The King of stock car racing, but he has a peer in Earnhardt, who shares his record of seven Winston Cup championships.

Dale's turned aside many a challenger since winning his first championship 17 years ago. Jeff Gordon merely is the latest threat to his reign.

I was happy driving for Bud Moore as far as driving for Bud Moore the person, but I wasn't comfortable with some of the other things that were going on. The opportunity came to get back together with Richard in '84, we signed our deal, and we just went that way ever since."

The Childress team has prospered by staying ahead of the curve. The team held together for 10 years almost unchanged. But as the veteran crewmen got older, Childress brought in others as good or better than those they replaced.

"If I had the same race team I had in 1986 and '87 going over the wall, I wouldn't be competitive," Childress says. "David Smith says he wants to come off the jack in a couple of years. But I've got a hell of a backup jack man, and David's working with him.

"That's the way I've structured this team. I've got plans for the future. I've got a lot of plans for Richard Childress Racing five years down the road."

Earnhardt knows Childress' plans may not always involve him.

"I think Richard's got people in mind to take over everybody's position," he says. "Who's his backup driver? I know he's got his eye on some people. People say, 'Doesn't that bother you?' No. It's Richard's priority; he's the car owner.

"It's just like me. All the people who work for me or are under me, I've got to perform and take care of them. I can't just go off in wonderland and forget about it. I've got to know what's going to happen in the future for these people who are involved."

The future for Dale Earnhardt may involve some new stretches of road, but he and Teresa already have demonstrated their ability to successfully negotiate uncharted terrain.

Ben Blake is a sportswriter for the *Richmond* (Va.) *Times-Dispatch*.

DARLINGTON
NASCAR
Goodwrench
MOM N' POP'S
Snap-on
FOOD CITY
GOODYEAR
AC
76
GM
Goodwrench Service
DUPONT
Winston Cup
Kellogg's Frosted Mini-Wheats
GMAC
Coca-Cola CLASSIC
Valvoline RACING
Jeff Gordon
Hendrick MOTORSPORTS
AC
PYROIL Racing
SIMPSON
Coca-Cola CLASSIC
DUPONT
AUTOMOTIVE FINISHES
GOODYEAR
DUPONT

PLEASE!
No Autographs
During Practice

NIGEL KINRADE

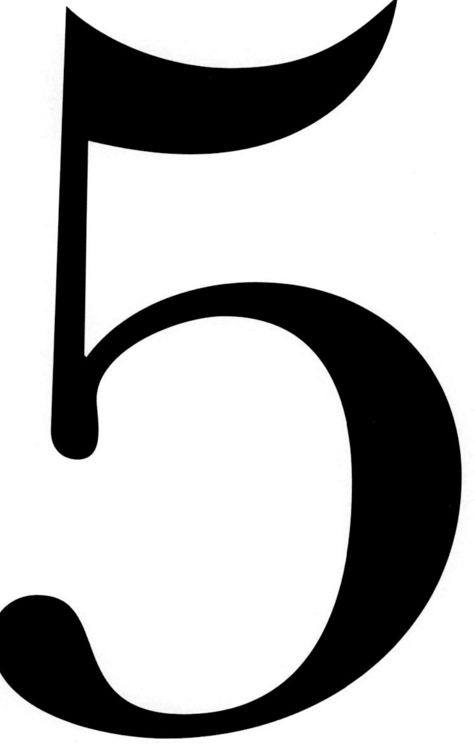

Wanted Man

He's self-made, sincere, loyal — and a winner. No wonder sponsors, corporations, media and fans want a piece of Dale Earnhardt.

By Steve Winzenread

During a Winston Cup season, Dale Earnhardt climbs into his race cars and chases the checkered flag 31 times.

Three times as often, or more than 100 times a year by conservative estimates, he makes a public appearance of some sort, sharing his considerable success and unique personality with fans and business people. Those paid get-

CHOBAT RACING IMAGES

togethers range from motivational speeches at conventions to autograph sessions to simply saying hello.

It's a byproduct of being not just a champion, but one of the sport's all-time greats whose life story offers inspiration and instruction.

There is nothing vanilla about Earnhardt. When he's introduced before a

Dale's first big corporate sponsor was Wrangler, which he joined at the end of the 1980 season.

race at the Charlotte Motor Speedway — located virtually in the backyard of his hometown of Kannapolis, N.C. — the response is emphatic, both in the adulation of his admirers and the disapproval of his detractors.

Whether it involves trading cards or his favorite soft drink, Dale chooses his endorsement

The same passionate reaction carries over to Earnhardt the corporate spokesman. From appearing on the QVC shopping network to making commercials for a soft drink, Earnhardt has clout. He can make the telephone ring, drawing eager buyers on the business end of the receiver. He can sell $1 million in merchandise in two hours on QVC, for example.

GEORGE TIEDEMANN / SPORTS ILLUSTRATED

ROB TRINGALI JR. / SPORTSCHROME EAST/WEST

Dale's list of endorsements is extensive, suggesting both how busy and how popular he is. GM-Goodwrench Service. Chevrolet. Snap-On Tools. Mom-n-Pop's. Western Steer. Gargoyles. Papa John's. BellSouth Mobility. Goodyear. Kellogg's. Sundrop. And more.

Ranked by Forbes magazine in 1997 as the eighth wealthiest athlete, Earnhardt has won more than $30 million during his racing career, and has parlayed that considerable amount into an even greater fortune.

No one handed Earnhardt his success, and his fans know it. His life is an object lesson in talent, perseverance and labor — all the ingredients embodied in the classic American dream. It makes him a natural to deliver motivational speeches.

"He talks about teamwork," relates John Rhodes, director of public relations, Winston Cup division, for Champion Sports Group. "He talks about being a champion and what it takes to be a champion."

That's a natural topic for Earnhardt, whose seven Winston Cup championships are equaled only by another racing legend, Richard Petty. Not coincidentally, Dale's success in pitching products also can be credited to doing

The partnership between Dale and GM-Goodwrench has been mutually beneficial, and Dale appears to be in it for the long haul.

__Dale hasn't always run with his now-famous No 3. In the early years, sponsors, and wins, were much harder to come by.__

what comes naturally.

Consider his television commercials for the Sundrop soft drink. In the first, he reminisces about drinking Sundrop as a child. It's a simple concept, but when you realize that the ad is filmed in the garage at the home in Kannapolis where Dale grew up, the emotional power is heightened. Then add the clincher: He's talking about his late father, Ralph, an accomplished racer in his own right

CHOBAT RACING IMAGES

who died of a heart attack in that very garage. The impact could not be more powerful or genuine.

"The best way to put it," says Tim Breiding, whose advertising agency handles sales promotions for Sundrop, "is it's always good when you have somebody who's a loyal customer of Sundrop to promote it. [Dale's] the epitome of a loyal Sundrop drinker. The neat thing about the TV spots is that they are

very real. It's just a natural fit."

Owing to his self-made story and his racing achievements, Dale is popular as a motivational speaker . . .

Being phony isn't part of Earnhardt's makeup, and that applies to his business decisions as much as his personality.

"He endorses things he enjoys," says Don Hawk, president of Dale Earnhardt Inc. "He endorses quality goods. He doesn't just endorse things for money. I've seen the man turn down things that were not in the best interest for himself, his sponsors or his sport. He won't endorse something just because they send him a paycheck."

SCOTT CUNNINGHAM

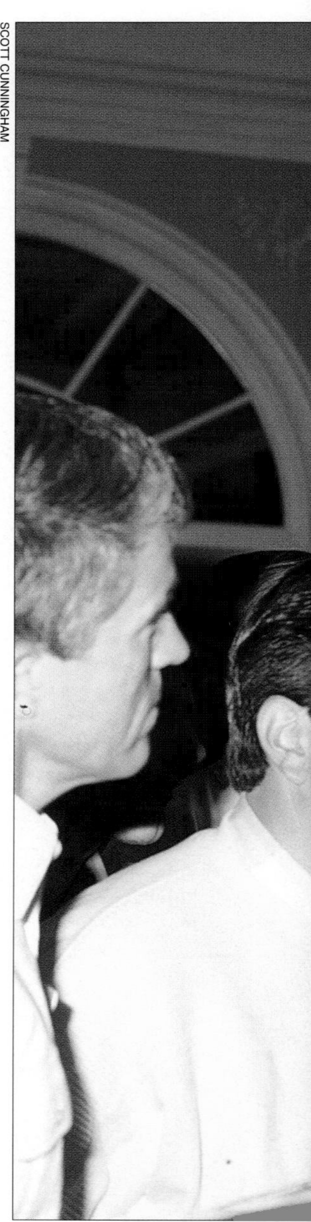

SCOTT CUNNINGHAM

When Earnhardt is racing, fans know they will see an all-out effort. He's the same way as a corporate representative.

"Except for a couple of personal weeks, every day he's involved in something for some sponsor," Hawk says. "Every day there's something that comes in that has to be dealt with, even if he's in the Bahamas. He doesn't get too many days free.

"He does everything from sign autographs, to question-and-answer sessions, to making speeches. On any given qualifying day, he'll have eight to 10 interviews. When he wins, it's just compounded. It's a good problem to have."

A few days after winning the Brickyard 400 at Indianapolis, Earnhardt shared with reporters a glimpse of his schedule.

"We had a little champagne with the crew after the race, went to the motorhome and cleaned up and then got a police escort to the airport," he said. "That was pretty impressive to get out of traffic so easily down the left lane and that stuff. It was fun riding to the airport.

"We got in the jet and flew to Carolina. We got there about 11:30 or 12:00 at night. We got a good night's rest and got up early the next morning. We have

. . . and as a public representative for companies such as GM-Goodwrench.

a lot of companies, and a lot of business goes on. I got on the airplane and flew to Nashville, went through Opryland and did some things there. I got to drive the No. 3 train.

"I was on *Music City Tonight.* Went out and had a great dinner. Flew back in to the Carolinas and started off again with the radio and press. We'll do Eli's (Gold) show and then have a dinner with some sponsors. Several things are planned for tomorrow, but one thing I've got to do is go to the [Chevrolet] dealership [in Newton, N.C.] and see the guys there."

SCOTT CUNNINGHAM

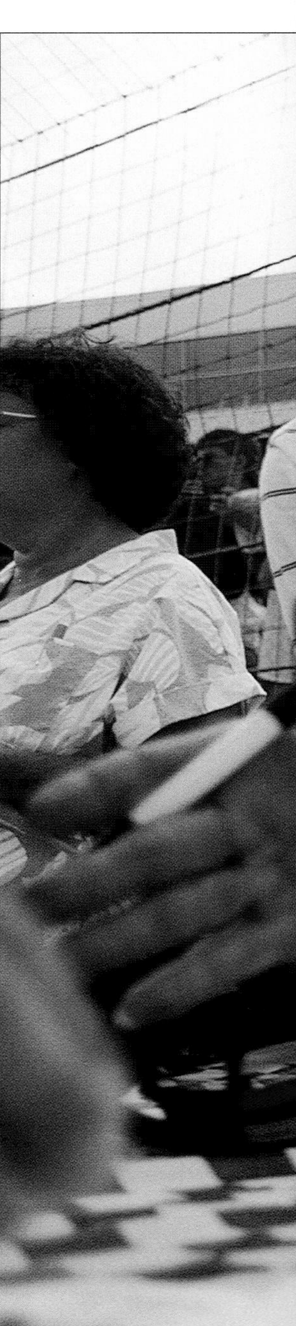

It seems Earnhardt's engine runs constantly. More than being just a pitchman, he's a savvy marketer, too, creating his own empire, one fueled by far more than just lucrative souvenir sales at speedways. Breiding says people may be surprised at Earnhardt the performer.

"He's fun to work with," Breiding says. "He's not as intimidating as you might think. He's a lot nicer guy than he's given credit for, and he's got a good management team, too. He's surrounded with good folks."

Many race fans perceive Dale as an intimidating figure, but those who've encountered him personally know he can be both accomodating and friendly.

Hawk, who is one of those "good folks," adds, "A lot of people are surprised at what a good corporate spokesman he is."

SCOTT CUNNINGHAM

Earnhardt's appearance with Jay Leno on *The Tonight Show* proves the point, Hawk says. "People are very surprised that what is supposed to be a Southern sport-only, backwoods-type race car driver can be so quick on his feet and so good on TV. A lot of that he has adapted throughout the years with his success."

You can only wonder how the younger Dale Earnhardt — the version that goes back 20 years and more — would have handled all of this notoriety. Today's version can banter with Leno and still make his point.

GM
Goodwrench

When Leno asked Earnhardt about his hometown, Dale informed his host that Kannapolis is "one of the biggest cotton mill towns in the country probably, with the Cannon [now Fieldcrest Cannon] mills. They named a street after me there, and had Dale Earnhardt Day there two years ago.

"Named a street after me," he continued. "Dale Earnhardt Boulevard. Same street they used to stop me for loud mufflers and maybe speeding a little bit, I don't know. That's amazing, isn't it? Things come around now, they've named the street after me."

In just a few words, Earnhardt defended and promoted his hometown, and boosted himself a little bit, too. Why not? Earnhardt's rise from school dropout to champion racer (and successful entrepreneur) is the stuff of self-

As Dale's record of achievements lengthened and his stature in the sport has grown, he has become a magnet for media of all types.

NIGEL KINRADE

sufficient American heroes through the ages.

A 24-page section published before Dale Earnhardt Day in *The Daily Independent* in Kannapolis proclaimed "Dale Earnhardt, Hometown Hero" on its front. When the daylong celebration was winding down with a fund-raiser on the night of Oct. 5, 1993, at the Kannapolis Country Club, Earnhardt was humble in his gratitude.

In September 1994 Earnhardt became the first Winston Cup driver to appear on* The Tonight Show. *He not only beat host Jay Leno around the parking lot in a tractor, he held his own in the on-air banter department.

People in Kannapolis, he said, "are my kind of people. Guys trying to make it on their own. They've got a tough row to hoe."

Speaking from the heart, he talked about his two brothers and two sisters helping him in the early, struggling days of his racing career, and of exhausting nights working when he would drop off to sleep, a wrench in his hand.

COURTESY OF MARGARET NORTON / NBC

"It took those long hours to make it," he said. "We'd argue all week long, and then we'd get to the racetrack and argue against everybody else.

"I had help from all these folks in Kannapolis," he added. "We did whatever it took. We'd get parts made at Cannon Mills and slip them out in a lunch box. All of these things got me to where I am.

"I want to thank all these folks," he continued. "I was scared to be honored by Kannapolis. I just drive race cars. But I've really been impressed and humbled today. Y'all have done a super job, and I'm super honored."

Even on that special night, his commercial career made an appearance when his sister, Kathy, teased him about another TV ad's tricycle racing premise (winner takes the soft drink). "You didn't get every Sundrop," she chided playfully.

Earnhardt, though, knows how to return a needle, as he did with Leno.

KANNAPOLIS (N.C.) DAILY INDEPENDENT

"You guys won an Emmy last night, didn't you?" Earnhardt asked. When Leno said yes, Earnhardt congratulated him, then posed another question: "How much does that pay?"

"The Emmys? That doesn't pay anything," Leno answered.

"It doesn't?" Earnhardt continued.

"No," Leno said. "You don't get any dough for that."

"Championships pay, like, a million-three, a million-four," Earnhardt countered.

Endorsements pay well, too. But only the ones Earnhardt is comfortable with. That's how he does business. The way a champion should.

Steve Winzenread is sports editor of *The Daily Independent* in Kannapolis, N.C.

When his hometown honored him with a Dale Earnhardt Appreciation Day in October 1993, Dale had no trouble returning the appreciation.

KANNAPOLIS (N.C.) DAILY INDEPENDENT

DAYTONA
50
40th A
EBRUARY
Coca-Cola
Snap-on
FOOD CITY
76
Coca-Cola
GM
Goodwrench
Service Plus
GOODYEAR
Goodwrench
Service
Winston
Coca-Cola

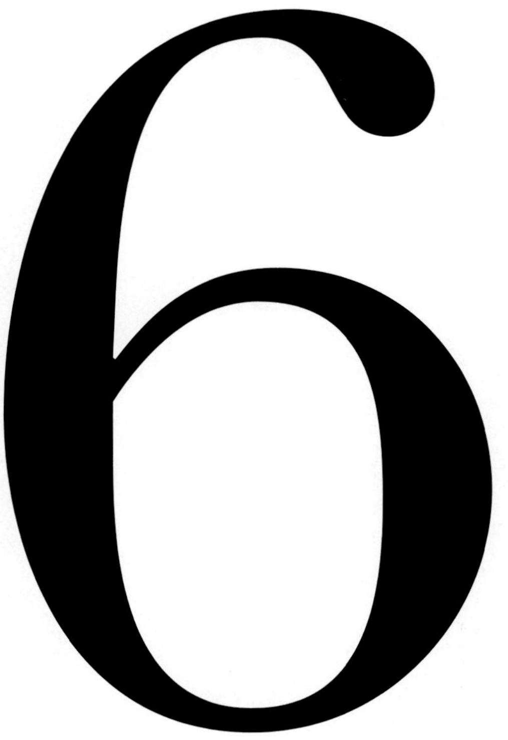

Duke of Daytona

Dale received the royal treatment from both friends and foes after his breakthrough win at the 1998 Daytona 500

By Mark Zeske

ALLEN KEE

Tide
PAYCHEX
EXIDE
Kodak
MAX
REALTREE
Skittles
Bud
LOWE'S
CORN FLAKES
Plus
Gatorade
125's

Dale Earnhardt stormed into the post-race interview session at the 1998 Daytona 500 armed with a stuffed monkey and a smile that stretched from ear to ear. With a flick of his wrist, The Intimidator sent the doll tumbling across the room, and off his back, if you will.

It wasn't that easy, but in his 20th attempt, Dale had finally won the Daytona 500.

In one of the most emotional finishes in Daytona history, Earnhardt held off a furious charge from Jeremy Mayfield, Rusty Wallace and Bobby Labonte down the stretch to win his first Daytona 500.

"Yes! Yes! Yes!" a jubilant Earnhardt shouted in victory lane. "Twenty years. Can you believe it?"

Earnhardt's victory celebration after his historic win was in full force just minutes after his No. 3 Monte Carlo crossed the finish line to the checkered flag.

There was Earnhardt, doing donuts through the Daytona logo on the grass section of the infield.

Earnhardt led the 1998 Daytona 500 five times, totaling 107 laps, more than any other driver. He took the lead for good on lap 140.

NIGEL KINRADE

There was Dale driving slowly down pit row, accepting the congratulatory hand slaps of a legion of admiring foes, many of whom had witnessed firsthand so many of the legend's near-misses at Daytona and could only cheer as Earnhardt sprayed Coke, Gatorade, champagne and several other NASCAR-sanctioned beverages over the throng in victory lane.

Less than an hour later, Earnhardt sat in the press box at Daytona International Speedway, monkey-less, sharing his views with media from all over world, while outside the party raged on. Earnhardt's victory was his 31st at the Florida track, including Winston Cup events, Busch races,

The No. 3 car must have seemed like a blur to Bobby Labonte and Rusty Wallace, who remained in close pursuit to the end but could never catch Earnhardt.

IROC all-star competitions, Twin 125 qualifiers and Bud Shootouts.

"I've won more races at Daytona than anybody in history, alive or dead," Earnhardt says. "I think that speaks for itself."

By the end of the 1997 season, many wondered if Earnhardt would even continue racing let alone ever visit victory lane again. There was a horrific wreck in July 1996 at Talladega that left him with a fractured sternum and collarbone, and a bizarre blackout in 1997 at Darlington at the beginning of the race. Earnhardt had finished fifth in points but had shocked the world by failing to win a race the entire year.

"By my standards," he says, "it was a terrible year."

It didn't help that many around him began questioning his decision to continue racing, trying tactfully to suggest that maybe it was time for The Intimidator to ride off into retirement while he still could.

Before winning the Daytona 500, Earnhardt hadn't won a Winston Cup points race since March 10, 1996, in Atlanta. The string of 59 consecutive starts without a victory is the longest such streak of his career.

Earnhardt believes that the two major moves of 1997, adding new teammate Mike Skinner and hiring Larry McReynolds as crew chief, are two of the biggest reasons he finally won the Daytona 500. And the first thing Earnhardt did when he jumped out of his car after the race was to hug McReynolds before turning to offer a high-five to Skinner, who had sprinted from his own race car to join in the celebration.

Even before the race, Dale had a good feeling. "I knew we had a good race car, and that's what's important," he says.

NIGEL KINRADE

"I don't know what [McReynolds] thought was going on after [1997]," Earnhardt says. "But he came back [in 1998] with the look in his eyes."

McReynolds, who earned a great reputation preparing the Fords of Robert Yates Racing, insists there was no lack of chemistry between himself and Earnhardt, a strong rumor through the Winston Cup grapevine during the troubled '97 season.

"I honestly think there was never a non-click between Dale and I," McReynolds says. "It was me understanding Chevrolets, understanding what Dale Earnhardt was looking for in a race car.

"It was a tough year last year, but nobody gave up. We kept pulling together, and it paid off."

ALLEN KEE

Earnhardt's friends and fellow drivers gathered around the winning car as Dale celebrated in victory lane.

Talk of the winless streak burned at Earnhardt, who believed that NASCAR hasn't given Chevrolet teams an even playing field against the Fords. For most of 1997, Jeff Gordon was the only Chevy driver to have a victory. But the negatives of '97 actually gave the Richard Childress team something to rally around.

"There's no doubt that we really started concentrating, really became focused, late [in 1997]," Earnhardt says. "I

NIGEL KINRADE

think the incident at Darlington sort of turned it around. It made us all take a step back and look at things real hard."

Dale's performance was also a big victory — a huge win — for Action Performance Companies. It was Action that bought Earnhardt's Sports Images company in the fall of 1996, also signing a preferred vendor license with the seven-time

The 1998 Daytona 500 was worth $1,059,150 to Earnhardt, making it the first NASCAR Winston Cup race with a purse of more than $1 million.

NASCAR
Winston
SERIES
Cup
7 Time Champion
Coca-Cola.
RCR
76
GM
Goodwrench
Service Plus
GOODYEAR
Winston Cup

ALLEN KEE

As Labonte and Wallace jostled for position down the stretch, Dale was able to pull away for one of the sweetest wins of his career.

Winston Cup champion. The deal not only gave Earnhardt a seat on the board at Action but gave the company many exclusive die-cast rights and the task of running his trackside souvenir business. Dale's win at Daytona put a new twist on the classic racing rule: "Whatever wins on Sunday, sells on Monday."

Earnhardt's souvenir rigs, which are operated by Action, were swamped after the race. The trailers were practically cleaned out. According to Action president Fred Wagenhals, sales at Dale's trailers were 27 percent higher that week than they had ever been at a Daytona race.

As Earnhardt was preparing for the rest of his career, he had only one thing in mind: another Winston Cup title.

"When I sit down in a race car, it's like the first day I ever did it," Dale says. "There's nothing else on my mind. I'm not sitting there while I'm racing pondering everything that's going on in my life. I'm just focused on beating whoever is in front of me or behind me."

Mark Zeske is the Senior Editor of *Beckett Racing & Monthly Marketplace.*

CHOBAT RACING IMAGES

Miles Behind, Miles Ahead

Dale Earnhardt has come a long way since his early days in Winston Cup racing, when he was on the other side of the fence from the stars of that era such as Richard Petty, Cale Yarborough, Bobby Allison and Darrell Waltrip. Now a seven-time champion, Dale is one of the circuit's most respected figures, an object of continuing devotion from his fans and, as always, a driver who's impossible not *to watch.*

NIGEL KINRADE

Fans may be used to seeing Dale barreling around a track in his black No. 3 Chevy, but a more familiar sight to his crew is Dale up to his elbows in an engine. That's one of the secrets to his success, and why he's a driver well worth keeping your eye on.

SCOTT CUNNINGHAM

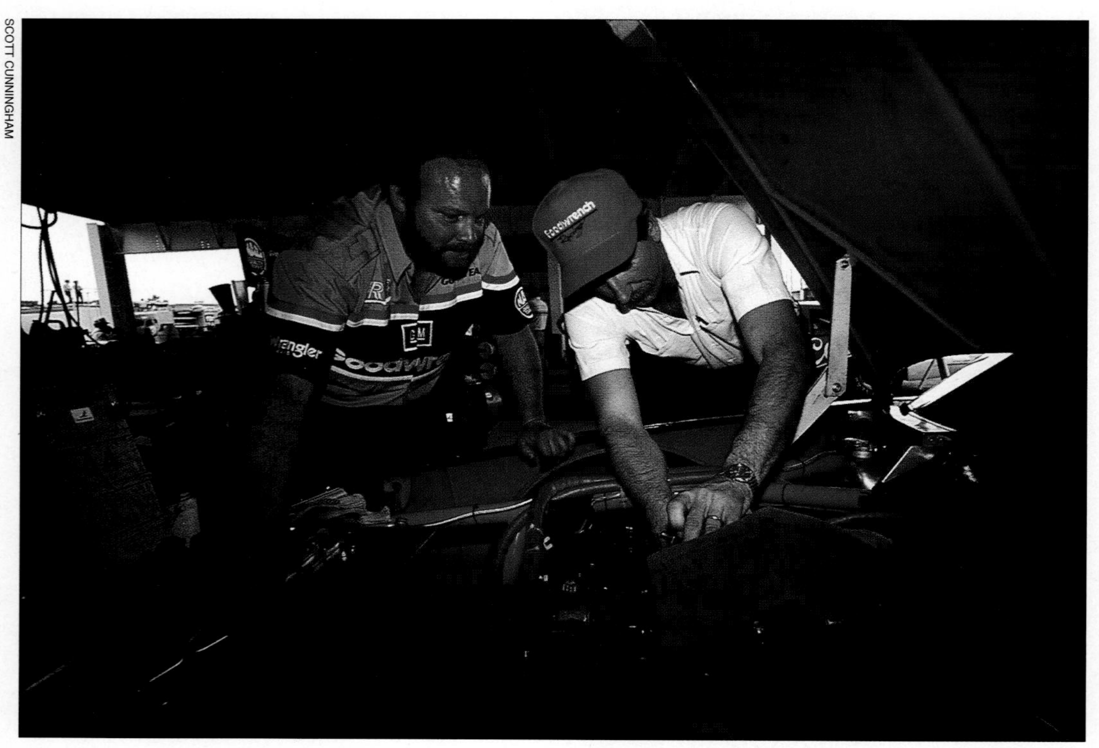

PAUL WEBB

EARNHARDT
BACK
IN
BLACK

SCOTT CUNNINGHAM

Win or lose, the Intimidator stirs the emotions of fans like no other. Sometimes scantily clad and always fiercely loyal to No. 3, Dale's worshippers have become legendary in NASCAR circles.

PAUL WEBB

DON GRASSMANN

GENE SWEENNEY JR.

NIGEL KINRADE

Whether it be T-shirts or painted nails, women have come up with unique ways to express their love for their favorite driver. With the influx of young Jeff Gordon and Rusty Wallace fans, devoted followers of Earnhardt have to find new ways of standing out.

24
DUPONT
THE
RULES

DON GRASSMANN

Earnhardt's most frightening accident came at the 1996 Diehard 500 in Talladega, when Dale tumbled down the first stretch, breaking his collarbone and sternum. What's left of the car is on display at the Richard Childress Racing Museum.

ROBERT ROGERS/SPORTS IMAGERY INC.

BRIAN SPURLOCK

BUSCH
Gatorade
Goody's
Holley
3M
JESEL
FOOD
GM
Snap-on
GOODYEAR
CHALLENGER
NASCAR

NIGEL KINRADE

DON GRASSMANN

Upon his courageous return to Talladega for the 1997 Winston 500, Dale found inspiring words from buddy Steve Waltrip. Earnhardt finished second, but remained fashion-conscious from head to toe.